Happy About™ Joint Venturing

The 8 Critical Factors of Success

By Valerie Orsoni-Vauthey

21265 Stevens Creek Blvd.
Suite 205
Cupertino, CA 95014

Happy About Joint Venturing: The 8 Critical Factors of Success

Copyright © 2006 by Happy About™

All rights reserved. No part of this book shall be reproduced, stored in a retrieval system, or transmitted by any means electronic, mechanical, photocopying, recording, or otherwise without written permission from the publisher. No patent liability is assumed with respect to the use of the information contained herein. Although every precaution has been taken in the preparation of this book, the publisher and author(s) assume no responsibility for errors or omissions. Neither is any liability assumed for damages resulting from the use of the information contained herein.

First Printing: June 2006
ISBN 1-60005-010-7
Place of Publication: Silicon Valley, California, USA
Library of Congress Control Number: 2006924557

Trademarks

All terms mentioned in this book that are known to be trademarks or service marks have been appropriately capitalized. Happy About™ cannot attest to the accuracy of this information. Use of a term in this book should not be regarded as affecting the validity of any trademark or service mark.

Warning and Disclaimer

Every effort has been made to make this book as complete and as accurate as possible, but no warranty of fitness is implied. The information provided is on an "as is" basis. The authors and the publisher shall have neither liability nor responsibility to any person or entity with respect to any loss or damages arising from the information contained in this book.

Publisher and Executive Editor

- Mitchell Levy, http://www.happyabout.info/

Cover Designer

- Malcolm Turk, http://www.flickerinc.com/

Layout Designer

- Val Swisher, President, Oak Hill Corporation http://www.oakhillcorporation.com/

Copy Editor

- Jennifer Finger, President, Keen Reader http://www.keenreader.com/

A Message From Happy About™

Thank you for your purchase of this Happy About book. It is available online at http://HappyAbout.info/jointventuring.php or at other online and physical book stores. The templates associated with this book can be picked up at http://HappyAbout.info/jointventuring/

- Please contact us for quantity discounts at sales@happyabout.info
- If you want to be informed by e-mail of upcoming Happy About™ books, please e-mail bookupdate@happyabout.info
- If you want to contribute to upcoming Happy About™ books, please go to http://happyabout.info/contribute/

Happy About helps companies establish thought leadership, increase leads and facilitate customer adoption. We write and publish books for corporations with a positive spin on educational and controversial topics utilizing case studies, testimonials and war stories from those that have "Been There and Done That!". Please contact us by e-mail sales@happyabout.info or phone (001-408-257-3000) if you are:

- A corporation that would like to explore having us create a book for you
- An author that would like to submit a book

Other Happy About books available include:

- Happy About LinkedIn for Recruiting: http://happyabout.info/linkedin4recruiting.php
- Happy About Website Payments with PayPal http://happyabout.info/paypal.php
- Happy About Outsourcing http://happyabout.info/outsourcing.php
- Happy About Knowing What to Expect in 2006 http://happyabout.info/economy.php

Other soon-to-be-released Happy About books include:

- Happy About CEO Excellence: http://happyabout.info/ceo-excellence.php
- Happy About Working After 60: http://happyabout.info/working-after-60.php
- Happy About Global Software Test Automation: http://happyabout.info/globalswtestautomation.php

Dedication

If you are like me I am sure you love reading the dedication page!

My first thanks go to Mitchell Levy for believing in this book since the first time I submitted this subject to him. Together, I am sure we will continue publishing great how-to books – stay tuned!

Second, my son Baptiste deserves a big pat on the back for being my inspiration and my sun when the sky is gray.

To my mom and my dad, I would like to send my love for being so supportive and for always believing in me.

To my beloved geek, thank you for spending late hours working with me on some mysterious bugs in Word.

And, last but not least, for his tireless efforts a big thank you goes to Michael Scadden, from MyPrivateCoach.com.

To all of you and to all my thriving business coaching clients, THANK YOU and TO YOUR SUCCESS!!

contents

intro	Introduction. 1	
Chapter 1	**The Right Partner**. **5**	
	What is a joint venture?. 6	
	How does a joint venture work?. 7	
	Should I start a joint venture?. 8	
	What are the risks involved?. 12	
	What are the legal implications of a joint venture?. . 14	
	Chapter 1 Highlights. 15	
Chapter 2	**Timing and Vision** **17**	
	Chapter 2 Highlights. 25	
Chapter 3	**Organization**. **27**	
	Time Management. 27	
	Working Process 30	
	Decision Process 36	
	Chapter 3 Highlights. 38	
Chapter 4	**Business Planning**. **39**	
	What is a Business Plan?. 41	
	Structure of a Business Plan 43	
	Starting Your Plan 44	
	Creating Your Business Plan 45	
	Chapter 4 Highlights. 63	
Chapter 5	**Human Resources and Skills Integration** . **65**	
	Assessing and recording skills 66	
	Managing skill gaps 69	
	Leveraging organization resources 70	
	Coaching employees or partners in	
	knowledge transfer. 72	
	Building and empowering teams 73	
	Attracting new talent and retaining your employees. 76	
	Protecting the people in your venture. 78	
	Chapter 5 Highlights. 81	

Chapter 6 | **Plan Execution. 83**

Execution Plan. 84
Time Management. 87
Organization. 92
Communication 93
Handling Frustration. 94
Staying Healthy 96
Chapter 6 Highlights. 98

Chapter 7 | **New Brand Marketing 99**

Product Marketing Strategies: Do You Need a New
Brand?. 100
Your Resources 105
Your Public Relations and Marketing Plan. 106
Chapter 7 Highlights. 121

Chapter 8 | **Exit Strategies - The End 123**

Being Acquired by a Parent Company. 123
Merging With Another Entity 124
Initial Public Offering (Going Public
With Your Business). 125
Sickness or Death of One or More of the Partners 127
Disagreement Between the Parties 129
The Joint Venture Missed Its Target
(Did Not Achieve Its Intended Goal). 130
Conclusion 132

Appendix A | **List of Outside Resources 135**

author | About the Author 139

intro

Introduction

If you can't beat 'em, join 'em. Two heads are better than one. United we stand. **If you are a business owner who wants to significantly increase market reach, break down barriers to entry in your market, or simply generate skyrocketing revenues in a shorter amount of time, these old adages are becoming more and more relevant.**

According to the Commonwealth Alliance Program (CAP), businesses anticipate strategic alliances accounted for 25% of all revenues in 2005, a total of 40 trillion dollars. This figure has been steadily growing over the past few years as more solopreneurs and Work At Home Parents (WAHPs) decide to unite to augment their odds of survival in a highly competitive global environment.

If you are an aspiring joint venturer who needs to acquire some key knowledge before making the decision to jump into this new world, or if you have already made the decision to start a joint venture but don't know where to begin, this "How-To" handbook is for you. Also, whether you seek funding or not, the information in these pages will give you the proper foundation for achieving your financial goals.

This book's mission will be two-fold: First, we will dive together into the technical aspects of joint venturing (JV), and I will give you the nuts and bolts of what a joint venture is and how to make yours successful. I am also going to expose some of the myths and realities of joint ventures so you can avoid the major pitfalls that are sometimes associated with this unique partnership. Second, I will cover the Eight Critical Factors of Success in the next eight chapters.

1. The Right Partner
2. Timing and Vision
3. Organization
4. Business Planning
5. Human Resources and Skills Integration
6. Plan Execution
7. New Brand Marketing
8. Exit Strategies – The End

As you go through these, I strongly recommend you keep a note pad handy and jot down all of the ideas that will inevitably come up.

If you are thinking about starting a JV yourself, draw two columns on a page. On the right side, put the essential elements for your JV to be a success, and on the left side, write your current situation. For instance, when I list the ideal traits for the right partner, compare them with your anticipated associate. This will help you determine the gap between required and available elements, how much work you need to achieve your goals and what difficulties lay ahead.

As you do your homework, write a business plan, look for and find a great partner and be ready to work hard towards achieving your goals. You will greatly increase your chances of success and be well on your way to an amazing and rewarding journey!

Are you ready to embark on this (joint) adventure together? It is time to get Happy About™ Joint Venturing!

chapter 1

The Right Partner

Seneca — "It's not because things are difficult that we dare not venture. It's because we dare not venture that they are difficult."

You are about to learn one of the most powerful tools I know of for being successful in today's competitive business atmosphere. I'm of course talking about Joint Ventures, or specifically, teaming up with another person, group of persons, or business entity for the purpose of expanding your business influence and creating a more powerful market presence.

In the following chapters, I will take the mystery out of what some consider to be a very complex subject and break it down into simplistic terms that are not only easy to understand, but more importantly, easy to implement for your own benefit.

Joint Ventures are in, and if you're not utilizing this strategic weapon, chances are your competition is, or will soon be, using this to their advantage.... possibly against you!

We hear of joint venture success stories every day in the media. Most are legitimate viable projects. However some, including ones you hear about on the Internet that promote strategic alliances that can make you rich overnight without a business plan, product, or service, are the ones to beware of. This book will teach you to recognize the pitfalls and give you the highest chance of success.

Our primary goal is to make you a successful joint venturer. This will happen if you are an informed entrepreneur. Thus, it is necessary for us to dive into the technical aspects of joint ventures. Specifically:

- **What is a joint venture?**
- **How does it work?**
- **Should I start a joint venture?**
- **What are my chances of success?**
- **What are the risks involved?**
- **What are the legal implications of a joint venture?**

What is a joint venture?

A joint venture is a strategic alliance where two or more parties, usually businesses, form a partnership to share markets, intellectual property, assets, knowledge, and, of course, profits.

A joint venture differs from a merger in the sense that there is no transfer of ownership in the deal.

This partnership can happen between goliaths in an industry. Cingular, for instance, is a strategic alliance between SBS and Bellsouth. It can also occur between two small businesses that believe partnering will help them successfully fight their bigger competitors.

Companies with identical products and services can also join forces to penetrate markets they wouldn't or couldn't consider without investing tremendous resources. Furthermore, due to local regulations, some markets can only be penetrated via joint venturing with a local business. In some cases, a large company can decide to form a joint venture with a smaller business in order to quickly acquire critical intellectual property, technology, or resources otherwise hard to obtain, even with plenty of cash at their disposal.

> The critical aspect of a joint venture does not lie in the process itself but in its execution.

How does a joint venture work?

The process of partnering is a well-known, time-tested principle. The critical aspect of a joint venture does not lie in the process itself but in its execution. We all know what needs to be done: specifically, it is necessary to join forces. However, it is easy to overlook the "hows" and "whats" in the excitement of the moment.

We will look at the "hows" in our review of the Eight Critical Factors of Success. For the moment, let's keep in mind that all mergers, large or small, need to be planned in detail and executed following a strict plan in order to keep all the chances of success on your side.

The "whats" should be covered in a legal agreement that will carefully list which party brings which assets (tangible and intangible) to the joint venture, as well as the objective of this strategic alliance. Although joint venture legal agreement templates can readily be found on the Internet, I suggest you seek the appropriate legal advice when entering such a business relationship.

Should I start a joint venture?

There is no straight answer to this question. The decision involves addressing various elements. Consider copying the following questions on a word processing document, so that you can constantly address and answer those important elements before and as you move forward.

Important questions to consider:

> **NOTE** Please use the template available at http://HappyAbout.info/jointventuring/

1. What do I sell, and how do I reach my target market?
2. Who are my competitors? If they are better at generating revenues and reaching the marketplace than me, what do they have that I don't?
3. Are there geographical areas that will remain beyond reach without local partners, or acquisition costs that are simply too high?
4. Do I need to develop a know-how, which has already been developed by a company or by an individual?
5. Is there a logical business partner that could help me develop a vertical or horizontal market penetration?

6. Do I have all the human resources I need in marketing, R&D, production, or operations? Is there a company I know which would have resources complementary to mine?
7. How do I feel about combining resources? Do I like to lead by myself and act as a solitary business hero, or am I fine with sharing the pie? Do I think it is better to own 20% of a $200 million company or 100% of a $1 million small business?
8. Do I have access to the right legal resources to structure the joint venture and insure all aspects are duly covered?
9. Are there local legal regulations I can bypass by partnering with a local business?
10. Do I have access to successful joint venturers who can share their experience with me?
11. Do I understand that going through the decision process entails sitting down and taking the time to write a full-fledged joint business plan?
12. Am I aware that in the vast majority of cases, merging activities, even when not necessarily identical, will result in an inevitable workforce reduction? How do I feel about letting go of some of my most faithful employees?
13. Am I looking at partnering because I don't see another way out of my current business problems? (Joint venturing should not be considered as a last resort action, but rather as one course of action among several others. This decision needs to be taken in a careful and methodical manner.)
14. Do I already know of a person or a company that I see has a real interest in partnering? Have I discussed this possibility with this person or with the person in charge of the

targeted company? If yes, what is the general feeling? If no, then it is time to start a high-level discussion to gauge the level of interest.

15. Is my company in need of more credibility? Do I know of a potential joint venture target, which has the level of credibility I am seeking?
16. What are my strengths and weaknesses? What are the threats and opportunities in my target market?
17. Do I have all the support I need to go through this major change in my business life? If I am going through personal turbulences, does it make sense to start such a major project?
18. What are my chances of success?

Although there are no official statistics on the rate of success of specific strategic alliances, like joint ventures, per se, a few studies have, however, been conducted in this field. Their main findings were that most joint ventures fail about 60% of the time within five years. Why? Experts agree that the key to success is the human factor, such as human resources integration and knowledge sharing, rather than geographical or financial factors.

> Most joint ventures fail about 60% of the time within five years.

Keep in mind that joint venturing in third world countries entails a higher rate of failure. Lack of local legal knowledge, communication problems, divergence on agreed-upon objectives, differing deadline perceptions, etc., all contribute to this elevated rate.

How do we measure the performance of a joint venture? There are several formulas that can be used. It depends on the strategic alliance in the first place. Do you wish to:

- Increase profits?
- Share R&D expenses?
- Extend or maintain market position?
- Improve distribution channels?
- Reduce overall costs/economies of scale?
- Develop new technology?
- Diversify product offerings?
- Reduce competition?
- Spread risk (mainly on large investments)?

Some of those goals are easily translated into financial figures like "percentage of increased profits," "who incurs which expenses," and "increased product offerings." For example, if you were planning to increase your profits by 20%, you just need to compare your achievements with your previous situation, and you will know with certainty how well your joint venture performed.

Though some objectives are hard to quantify, like "reducing competition," for instance, methods are always available to analyze how well a joint venture's plan was executed. One could argue that if competition is cut down, then profits should increase.

If reducing competition has the sole objective of stabilizing or reversing a slowing revenue growth, it is easy to demonstrate the positive impact a strategic alliance could have on such a goal.

Remember, the key determining element responsible for joint venture failures is the human factor. Being able to make your employees feel comfortable about a potentially disturbing strategic alliance will be crucial to your success. This implies that not only must both sides understand how much they have to gain from this joint venture, but more importantly, how much they can lose by not partnering.

Information sharing will be vital, and it is essential that as early as possible, both teams talk and exchange their knowledge. This entails meetings, steering committees, joint company events, employee "swaps" and internal promotions.

Going back to our primary question: what are my chances for success? We know that on average, only about 40% of joint ventures are successful within five years. Since this figure includes partnerships with underdeveloped countries; which have a high rate of failure, we can reasonably state that if you join forces with a company located in a developed area and have done your homework, your probability of success should be closer to 80%.

What are the risks involved?

Because strategic alliances are built on trust and convergent goals, one of the main risks you can face may occur if the partners are from different cultures. They may not trust operating a certain "way" or have divergent goals. Even with similar strategic goals, two partners who lack trust in each other may lack the willingness to reciprocate. When joint venturing, be prepared to give and take.

This sharing principle should govern the entire process. Many potential joint ventures, including large-scale projects, have died before the ink on the contract was dry, because of divergent goals and self-serving attitudes, which are not in synch with the essence of the joint venture. One example of this was the British Aerospace/Taiwan Aerospace alliance. After tough negotiations, the two parties signed an agreement during a celebrated ceremony in Taiwan. Soon after, Taiwan announced its wish to pull out of the deal. Why? Because their goals were divergent. Taiwan wanted to acquire new technology, which the British refused to give away, and the British wanted to capture new markets in Asia, which Taiwan refused to grant.

A joint venture concept is only effective when there is a true willingness to move forward together. Not even signed contracts have value if mutual trust and acceptance of the terms are not present. It is actually better not to consider a joint venture project if motives from either side are questioned by the other side. A graceful exit before any legal obligation takes effect will most likely prevent an inevitable failure.

The risks involved are therefore simple to evaluate. You can:

- Waste your time
- Lose money
- Let go of important technology
- Gain nothing of significance in return
- Squander your credibility

Even though these and other risks in joint ventures are present, the rewards can far outweigh pitfalls. It is important to completely evaluate your risks, and do your homework before and during the process.

What are the legal implications of a joint venture?

The geographical locations of the partners and target markets involved will dictate the degree of legal complexity when joint venturing.

If you both operate in the United States, you will need to sign at least one document: a joint venture agreement. Because of the rapid evolution of legislation, I strongly suggest you seek the proper legal advice, rather than using a pre-made template that is readily found on the Internet or in books.

If one of the partners is not located in the United States, or if both parties are foreign, additional documents will need to be signed: specifically, a New Legal Entity and a Joint Venture Agreement. Also, in some countries where local market access is restricted, you will have to go through a local "Validation" of your privileges and of the status of your joint venture.

Again, there are always legal variances depending on the goals and scope of your joint venture. I cannot stress strongly enough to go through the proper legal channels and seek comprehensive professional advice.

Chapter 1 Highlights

- A joint venture is a strategic alliance where two or more parties, usually businesses, form a partnership to share markets, intellectual property, assets, knowledge, and, of course, profits.
- A joint venture is different from a merger, where transfer of ownership is part of the deal.
- You have an 80% chance of success when starting a joint venture, if you do your homework and follow the steps outlined in this book.
- The major determining factor of success or failure in a joint venture lies within the human factor. By putting the right people in the right positions, you greatly augment your chances for achieving your goals.
- Seek legal advice, especially if you are targeting a foreign market.

Chapter 2
Timing and Vision

Henry David Thoreau

"Men are born to succeed, not fail."

Joel Barker

"Vision without action is a dream. Action without vision is simply passing the time. Action with vision is making a positive difference."

Have you already launched your joint venture with a partner? How did it happen? Were you in a hurry to start right away?

More often than not soft joint ventures are created in the heat of the moment by partners who can clearly see that this endeavor is a sure path to success.

Joint venturers don't always take the time to work on a business plan, which we will study in chapter 4 together. Even when they do so, partners assume that all parties are on the same page when it comes to the general vision and timing of the venture. This is a critical mistake that can lead to failure.

A joint venture is not a "traditional" company where a CEO drives the team. In a joint venture, as commonly understood today, both partners have technically the same power. Because both partners can pull the company at the same time, it is important that your sense of timing be the same.

What do I mean by "timing" and "vision," and why are they so important?

Charles R. Swindoll — "With vision there is no room to be frightened. No reason for intimidation. It's time to march forward! Let's be confident and positive!"

Let's answer the following questions:

NOTE Please use the template available at http://HappyAbout.info/jointventuring/

- Do you want to make $1 million within the next 6 months?
- Does your partner want to make $10 million within 12 months?
- Do you want this to be a side business?
- Does he/she want this to be a huge company?
- Do you want this to be your ticket to retirement?

Homework

- Organize a session with your partner and answer those questions together, on a separate sheet of paper. Once you are both done, compare your answers.
- Do not waste your time on "neatness" and "perfect wording." What matters here is the content, not the form.
- Write by hand, if at all possible. We have seen better results when people write with their hands, as if having a direct connection with the paper to translate one's thoughts and feelings would help being more "honest" with oneself.

You can easily imagine that if your wish is to build a side home-based business, while your partner is after the next big thing with office space and a large team, you will be confronted with a **vision alignment issue**, which can easily become a major problem if not tackled early on.

One way to address this quandary-assuming you still want to continue together because the business model and the market appeal to you-is to divide the work load in the most efficient way. This may imply a heavier involvement from your partner's side; which could be compensated by a higher stake in the joint venture.

This "middle-approach" is the optimal way to guarantee both sides will not be frustrated by what seems to be an unequal investment of time and energy: either because one partner is (apparently) not working enough, or because one partner is putting too many hours in this venture which can generate a feeling of guilt in the other.

Differences in ambition levels can also unleash unexpected conflicts if not dealt with early on. Though related to "vision" or "timing," ambition is a completely different concept. Indeed, ambition implies a striving after something higher than oneself. It can mean achieving personal, professional, or familial goals that are beyond the reasonably accepted ones, or beyond what we think society expects from us. In a joint venture, ambition to succeed is a key to success, as it will be the energy that will fuel the partners in times of difficulty. It is perfectly fine that the partners' ambition levels may not be aligned, as long as the differences are acknowledged and accepted. Usually, the most ambitious of the partners will be the one in the leading role, e.g. CEO, Sales, Business Development, etc., while the other partner will do wonders in equally important but more discrete functions, such as R&D. The best situations are achieved when there is actually a difference in ambition levels which is recognized by all the key parties in the joint venture. Ego-based conflicts are less likely to happen in those situations.

An exception to this is when the joint venture involves two existing companies, each with its own structure. In this particular situation having two ambitious leaders will allow for a higher likelihood of success.

> **Your Homework**
> Please use the template available at http://HappyAbout.info/jointventuring/
> - Have both partners define their ambition level: you can name this (like a "regular company" would):
>   – your goals
>   – your mission on earth
>   – your higher vision
> - Compare your answers. You can combine this exercise with the above-mentioned homework.
>
> Acknowledge any differences between your ambition levels and accept them. Understanding and accepting your differences is key to your success.

Both these subjects naturally lead to the level of commitment, i.e. committed time the partners want to have in the venture.

From your vision of the venture it will be an easy task to determine how much time each party is willing to invest:

- side business managed from home will mean less time spent on the venture
- the "ticket" to retirement approach will most likely mean long days spent on starting and growing the venture

Though it is quite possible to handle an uneven condition with one party working more than the other, it is a more difficult situation when one partner modifies his or her time commitment in the process of growing the venture.

Both partners will have to agree from the onset on how much time each party will commit. If a future evolution is expected, it should be acknowledged as early on as possible. Make sure you have fully discussed your private life with your JV partner: how much support you are receiving, how much stress you are going through (divorce, health issues, problems with family, etc.). Disclosing as much as possible will help ease understanding in times where you can not be fully focused on the venture.

Take this quote from John Naisbitt: "Strategic planning is worthless-unless there is first a strategic vision." Make it "Strategic planning is worthless-unless there is first a joint strategic vision." This will be the continuing driving force behind your growth.

"Don't look for life balance in the first few months."

Homework

Please use the template available at http://HappyAbout.info/jointventuring/

- Take a piece of paper and write your answers to the following questions:
  - How much time are you ready to invest in this venture? If you anticipate an evolution in your time commitment, indicate it here.
  - Do you think you both have the same sense of urgency?
- Validate your answers with your life partner. If necessary, revise them so that you can count on your life partner's support in all circumstances. Not being in agreement on how much time you are ready to invest in the venture, for instance, may lead to conflicts in your life, which is not the best way to succeed. That being said, we have seen joint venturers succeed even though they were receiving no support whatsoever from their life partner.
- Once you feel comfortable about your answers to those two critical questions, share them with your partner. Match your respective time commitment with your responsibilities within the venture: do you have a gap? If you do, talk with your partner to find a way to cover the responsibilities which are left uncovered. Do the same for your respective senses of urgency.

This exercise, though easy, fast and straightforward, will truly help you take the right steps to acknowledge differences in "vision and timing" perception.

As the founder of MyPrivateCoach, the leading coaching organization in the United States and in Europe, I am often asked by clients and journalists alike: "How can one keep a balanced life when starting a business or a joint venture?" The answer is simple: "Don't look for life balance in the first few months." Trying to be successful on all fronts at all times is a source of frustration as we discover that this will simply not happen. Understand right away that for a few months your family may not see you as much as in the times "before." It may seem a hard decision to make, but if you involve your family in the project, then this becomes a family success, and you won't have to justify how much time you are spending on this joint venture. Once you have understood that concept, you will be equipped with what you need to start a successful business: freedom to work as much as you need.

However, keep in mind two important elements:

- You do not want to overwork yourself, or you will run the risk of burning yourself out, which would definitely prevent you from reaching your goals. Make sure your partner does not overwork him/herself either.
- After the first few months will come the hardest part of all: letting go of it. Learn to progressively come back to a balanced life. Take the time to share quality time with the ones you love. Learn to delegate more. After six months, your venture should be able to do without your working weekends and nights. The same applies to your partner. If this is not the case, revise your human resource planning and hire the necessary profiles.

Homework

- Decide to keep track of how much you work, and keep one day per week away from your E-mails/computer/professional phone.
- Decide on a specific date on which you will let go of the "crazy startup days" and resume a balanced life. Put this in a visible place and hold on to it. Your commitment to yourself and your family is as important as the one you have to your business.

Chapter 2 Highlights

- In Chapter 1, we were looking for the ideal partner, examining all facets of potential perfect profiles. However, as you are now aware, having a partner aligned with your strategy is not enough. Finding the best business partner may be a long, time-consuming process. Spending time making sure your vision and timing are aligned may apparently slow your progress, but this will make the difference between a hard journey to your goal and a swift ride to success.

chapter 3
Organization

Ted W. Engstrom

"Anything that is wasted effort represents wasted time. The best management of our time thus becomes linked inseparably with the best utilization of our efforts."

Successful organization is a Critical Factor of Success, as it guarantees you are making the most of your time.

Organization covers:

1. Time Management
2. Working Process
3. Decision Process

Time Management

You cannot discuss the subject of organization or become better organized without learning time management skills. Understand that the concept of being able to manage time is a fallacy. You cannot manage time. You can only manage yourself. Everyone has twenty-four hours in a day. How you use that time will determine to a large extent what kind of success you will have in both your career and your life.

I touch on the subject of time management in discussing organization because both are closely linked; i.e. it is difficult to be organized without having excellent time management skills. We will take a more exhaustive view, with tips and examples of how to utilize your time more effectively, in chapter 6.

For the purpose of this section, let's go over the top twelve mistakes people make when it comes to managing their time. They are:

1. Wanting to do too much in too little time
2. Trying to remember everything (as opposed to writing down everything in a "store and forget" approach)
3. Letting incoming emails pollute your mind
4. Letting unexpected visits ruin your organization
5. Wasting your time on the Internet browsing unnecessary pages
6. Confusing "being active" with "delivering"
7. Lack of efficient prioritizing
8. Letting any type of distraction impact your work (listening to the radio while working is a good example)
9. Always saying "yes" to any request
10. Jumping from one task to the other without having completed the first one
11. Always working on what is more attractive to you (and not what is most critical to your business)
12. Not allowing yourself to breathe, relax, and re-energize yourself between major tasks

Homework

Please use the template available at http://HappyAbout.info/jointventuring/

- Look at the top twelve mistakes and check to see how well you perform. For each mistake write a full sentence. For instance: (12) Yes, I feel guilty if I stop, stand up from my chair and go for a 10-minute walk even if I have completed a major task; or (7) No. I prioritize everything I need to do. I even re-order my list every morning.

    By going over each and every line, you will find areas for improvement, and also don't forget to congratulate yourself for all traps in which you don't fall into.

- For each mistake you are making, decide on a course of action and implement it right away. If you have a problem with E-mails, i.e. you let incoming E-mails dictate your work, then decide to turn off your send/receive function for two hours. You will be impressed by how much you can accomplish when no disturbing message arrives while you are busy thinking! Your goal is to have a "clear" list of mistakes by the end of next week. Give yourself about ten days to fully control your time management "saboteurs."

Working Process

When you partner either with an individual or with a company, you will have to modify your working habits, not necessarily because they were wrong or inefficient, but because your processes may be redundant with those of your new partner, or because your working habits are not "compatible."

Tom Greening

"All time management begins with planning."

You may also need to re-adjust your working hours, how many times a week you commute to work, how much you work from home and how much you interact with your partner.

Make sure you both understand each other's way. Here are a few things you want to work on:

- **Level of structure in the entity.** Some like to be highly structured in their work and document all they do. This usually ends up in piles of supposedly needed procedures. Beware not to suffer from the Fortune 500 syndrome! While large corporations work on lightening their process, try not to make yours too heavy. Small companies need to be responsive; as this is where their main advantage lies. Not behaving as a mammoth is your key to success. Some people will feel more comfortable with a total lack of structure. While this can fly with a solopreneurship, it will make you fail if you don't straighten up your business processes. It is important to document the basic, albeit critical, functions of your company. Not knowing where the stamps are is okay, but not knowing where to find the key accounting documents is not. The purpose of lightly documenting your processes is to ultimately save your precious time. Why re-invent the wheel each time you repeat a task?

Homework

- **Streamline your process**. Adopt each side's best practices. Train your respective teams to adopt the new organization.
- Though it may sound hard, you will **need to agree on the level of structure and organization** your new entity will have. The best way to do so is to get together with your partner, spend a few hours presenting your respective ways and deciding which ones are most efficient. For instance, you may use a very structured approach for new employee hiring, which has proved to be effective for you, while your partner may have used a very loosely documented approach. For liability and efficiency reasons, you may want to opt for the more structured one.

- **Communication.** It is important that you organize your communication in the same way so as not to perturb your "joined" teams (or even yourself). If one partner sees the world in a half-empty way, and the other one in a half-full manner, go for the positive approach.

  This may mean spending some necessary funds on management and communication training, but this will be money well spent. So much energy can be wasted. So many failures occur due to miscommunication. So many problems can arise due to a lack of understanding of dissimilarities in communication style due to cultural differences.

  As the initiators of the ventures, you will have to teach by example. Make sure you implement the following suggestions, as listed in "Your Homework."

Your Homework

- Teach your employees how **to communicate positively**.
- Never "attack" anybody in an E-mail sent to more than one person. Public humiliation is the worst feeling, and the damage is very hard to repair.
- Formulate your sentences so that you project positivism. (Bad example: "We only achieved this much and John did not deliver on time." Good example: "We achieved x, below our expectations, but all is being done to exceed our next months quote. Report AXZ was not delivered in May as planned, but we have set a new firm date: June 16th, 2006.")
- If there are cultural differences within the newly formed teams, **train all members** to avoid any misunderstanding. For instance, in some cultures it is rude to use the informal subject form, like "tu" in Spanish or French, with a manager. In some other cultures, you never name a person alone but rather you put forth the entire team, etc.
- Keep **communication as its highest level** at all times. Send updates about how well the company is performing, market analyses, and welcome messages to new employees. Celebrate your success by sharing it with the entire team. Even if your group is small, it deserves to be informed. Even if it is only the two of you, ensure yourself that your partner is kept in the loop as much as you can.
- Though good, sound, and organized communication is key, structure it enough **so that your exchanges are not overwhelming**, and don't waste your time over needless E-mails or phone conversations.

- **Workspace organization and localization**. Until joining forces, you may have had teams scattered around the globe: e.g., development teams in Asia or Eastern Europe, customer support in Ireland or assistants in various cities in the United States. Your partner may be in the same situation, but using resources in other locations. You will have to define which teams are best to keep as is, and which teams should be merged, suppressed or expanded. To make this decision, your best bet is to run a cost analysis on each structure, and keep the ones which have the least impact on your bottom line. Once you have decided on which teams you keep where, align their business process or workflow. This will unquestionably require some training to bring your new teams up-to-date, but it will significantly help you save funds.

Being a leader may mean, at times, not being loved by all.

> **Homework**
> - Define your resources. Completely define size and localization. Run a cost analysis for each group. Show their impact on your bottom line. Extrapolate the impact expanded or reduced teams would have on your results, e.g. image problems, quality issues, training to develop, communication concerns, etc.
> - Prepare a decision document which will show different alternatives.
> - Decide, inform, communicate and implement. Launch training sessions if needed.

If you do not have teams around the globe or around your country, but simply have two or three people working for you, then your task will be easier. Just define their work procedures, and see if all your basic needs are covered. If you find redundancies, eliminate them. If you now have two persons fulfilling the same tasks, re-allocate one resource on other tasks.

One thing you will want to avoid is being too indulgent in keeping parallel processes in order to not hurt people's feelings. You are a leader. You need to make decisions even if in the short term this means cutting off workload or removing power from your employees' hands.

Many joint venturers face this problem as they strive to please everyone. This is not your path to victory. Keeping everybody in a shaky status-quo will not make your new company a winner. Being a leader may mean, at times, not being loved by all.

Decision Process

You were alone; now it is the two of you. You had one team; now you have two teams formed as one. You were small, and you became big.

David Coblitz

"A committee can make a decision that is dumber than any of its members."

You used to make your decisions without consulting anybody, but now you have to ask somebody else's opinion before deciding on any important matter for your company.

How do you cope with this situation? Are you bothered? Are your feelings hurt? Has your decision-making process been slowed? Or on the contrary, are pleased with this 'new order'?

No matter what your decision process was or is, it will now impact your business on a larger scale. You absolutely need to put in place decision processes where:

- **All parties involved** have their say.
- You establish a **clear end** (deadline) to any negotiation or presentation you may need to work on to reach a consensus.
- You institute a well defined **group of people empowered** to decide on specific topics. For example: John and CEO can decide on anything related to suppliers, CEO & VP BizDev can decide on all related new partnerships, etc. Not being the only person signing off on major decisions will definitely help you avoid the main traps in a joint venture. But again, a lack of clearly defined

decision-making processes, which worked in a solopreneurship, will NOT work in a joint venture.
- **All emotions and attitudes** about the particular decision will have been taken care of, and either integrated in the process or eliminated. This will help get the majority buying into the final output.
- The **end result** (the decision) is perceived by the decision-makers and the group as the **soundest**, given the time, circumstances and desired outcome.
- **The decision leads to a positive outcome**: better performances, superior products, healthier employees, more motivated teams, improved ROI, etc.

Homework
- Write your decision-making process. Allow for the unexpected. Maybe a decision-maker is absent, timing is altered, etc. The output is a procedure signed off by all decision-makers within the new organization, i.e. the joint venture.
- Inform your team about the new procedure. Share it. Explain it. Make it visible. In short, communicate.

As you now know, organizing your new forces into a new structure is a key factor of success. Not retaining too many "old ways" will allow your joint venture to exist by itself, without being weighed down by processes from the past. Furthermore, re-creating your organization and shuffling your teams around will create a new feeling, a new attitude, and a new "joint venture person" whose future is written with the ink of the new organization, not with the hopes of the old one.

In the end, you want a new homogeneous joint venture: highly motivated, informed, committed, organized, structured and trained.

To your success!

> ## Chapter 3 Highlights
>
> The organizational aspects of your new venture are key success factors and should never be overlooked. The three areas you will have to focus on are:
>
> 1. Time management
> 2. Working process
> 3. Decision process
>
> Joint venturers on a shoestring budget tend to try to do everything and accept an excessive level of workload. Poor time management is a reason for failure as starting and growing a joint venture is like running a marathon, not a 60-yard sprint.
>
> Combine your working processes and fine-tune them until you feel you have a homogeneous process that will be accepted by both parties.
>
> Taking quick and smart decisions without unnecessary lengthy meetings is vital in our competitive world. Organizing your new structure to fulfill this need should be one of your top priorities.

chapter 4

Business Planning

old Venture Capitalist's saying

"On a scale of 1 to 10, an idea is worth 1, the motivation to move forward is worth 5 and business planning is worth 10."

If you plan on launching a full-scale joint venture, i.e. not a side project, a business plan will be a key to your success. A full-scale joint venture is an enterprise which will use the major part of your resources, and should eventually make the bulk of your earnings.

If you are engaging in a "soft" joint venture, you may just need to run a few figures on a piece of paper, and your decisions will be easily made. A soft joint venture is a side project that you enter for a specific business and sometimes, for a limited time.

You can take classes on business planning, but the best way to work on a business plan is to stop, turn off your cell phone and pager, close Outlook and your instant messenger, and focus for a few hours on this chapter. What you will find in this chapter is insider knowledge from my years spent in the banking and venture world. You will know what investors like to see and what they'd rather not have to read. Here are the "do's and don'ts of business plan writing."

> ### Prepare Yourself
> Please use the template available at http://HappyAbout.info/jointventuring/
> - Have a note pad handy, or open a new word processing document on your computer.
> - Make sure you have all relevant information regarding your venture within easy reach: names of parties involved, figures, definitions, earlier plans, contacts, etc.
> - Isolate yourself. Do not let any disturbance prevent you from being 100% focused.
> - Start alone to allow for your full attention and avoid lengthy discussion. Do not hesitate to leave blanks. You will fill them in when you meet with your partner(s).
> - If you have questions, write them down on a "Questions List." You will find the time to address them later on.

Keep one thing in mind. The subject of business planning is very involved. This chapter will give you an excellent jump start, but can in no way give you all the necessary details that can make or break your chances for funding.

For a more an in-depth look at how to create the best possible plan for your business, be sure to check out our business boot camp at www.myprivatecoach.com. It is the best guide I know for writing what potential investors look for, and the daily lessons (via E-mail) really help you to stay on track.

What is a Business Plan?

A **business plan** is a document that summarizes the operational and financial objectives of a business. It contains the detailed plans, forecasts and budgets showing how the goals are to be achieved. Having an objective is not enough; you need to be prepared for all the intermediary steps. For anyone starting a full-scale business (whether in a joint venture or not), working on business planning is a vital first step.

Paula Nelson, successful entrepreneur, best-selling author and journalist at CNN Business News

"The best business plans are straightforward documents that spell out the "who, what, where, why, and how much."

Even if you are not looking for funding and you do not need to present your company to anybody but you and your partner, writing a business plan will still be of great, if not critical, value.

Why?

A business plan is the safest and cheapest way to test the feasibility of your business idea, and it allows you to get to know the market well before launching a new product or service.

Your business plan is a thorough analysis of all the facets of your business. Writing this document will force you to cover all the subjects; even the ones you don't like or with which you do not feel comfortable.

It is completely normal to feel uneasy with some subjects because we all have our fortes as well as our weaknesses. The key here will be to find the right resource to help you write and study the parts you are not comfortable with. Typically, your partner should be the one who feels at ease with the uncomfortable areas of the business plan!

There is one additional important reason why a business plan is so useful and critical. It will force you to prioritize and allocate your resources to the items which really make sense from a financial perspective. For instance, I had a client, who spent, against my advice, over $2,000 on a business program, which was supposed to make her rich effortlessly and fast. This is usually too good to be true, and needless to say, she ended up spending $2,000 on an Internet-based business, which has never generated any income for her. Had she taken the time to write a business plan, she would have seen beforehand that this would not be a successful endeavor.

Writing a business plan may sound scary at first, but it is not necessarily a time-consuming task. For soft ventures, just going through the major parts of the plan will have you reflect upon the key aspects of your partnership. You will not need to write 50 pages in this case. For full-scale ventures, then yes, you will need to do your share of thinking and writing to structure your ideas. However, sooner than you think, you will be grateful you took the time to go through such an exercise.

> **Important Elements**
> - A business plan is your flight plan. It succinctly lists who, what, where, when, why and how. Without a flight plan, a pilot cannot fly from point A to point B. The same applies to an entrepreneur.
> - When trying to get funding for your company, the difference between an investment proposal and a business plan is not a tremendous amount. It used to be different, when investors were "easy" in giving would-be entrepreneurs the necessary funds. Now, venture capitalists want more details and are more risk-averse. If you have a good, sound business plan, it can serve both purposes without a problem. The major difference will be found in the appendices where more financial statements will be presented.

Structure of a Business Plan

While the layout and the titles may vary from one document to another, you will always find the same type of information. In essence, the business plan will cover:

- **What you plan to offer**
- **How you plan to offer it**
- **If the market is ready for it**
- **How much competition you are expecting**
- **Who you are and what your experience is in that field**
- **Do you have a team?**
- **How much structure you already have in place**
- **Your operation plan**
- **Your exit strategy**

One point, which is most significant for investors, is how you plan to end the business. This is called the exit strategy. Exit strategies are formal details of how a company will be dissolved. It can also mean a change in structure. For example, an IPO (Initial Public Offering –when a company gets listed on the stock market) or an acquisition are both changes in legal structure, in which the original business will have to go through a process of dissolution in order to adopt the new legal entity.

In each case, the original structure is ended; you exit from responsibility.

Starting Your Plan

One important part in your business plan will be the Executive Summary. This is usually the first section of your plan. However, you will write it only when you have completed all your work. This, as its name indicates, will present the essence of your business. The idea is to make this summary attractive enough for a busy investor to be willing to spend an hour or more reviewing it and be interested enough to fund your venture.

Note that your business plan outline will differ on two factors:

1. **Type of Business**: Details of critical success factors for businesses in your industry must be included in the plan. Technology companies will discuss research and development, intellectual property, and time-to-market. A retailer will feature pricing methods, inventory control,

merchandising, and location. Ensure that your plan is comprehensive by addressing factors important to your industry.
2. **Type of Audience**: A banker's business plan will be different from an investor's, a partner's or a solopreneur's. Bankers like to see risk assessment and planning, loan amounts, repayment terms and collateral. Investors want a return on investment, an exit strategy, and planned growth with the funds. Partners need to understand what's in it for them, and a solopreneur likes to see where she is going with her company.

Creating Your Business Plan

There are ten main sections in a business plan:

1. Name of the Company
2. Mission
3. Executive Summary
4. Company Description
5. Presentation of Products and/or Services
6. Marketing and Sales
7. Operations
8. Management
9. Financials
10. Conclusion

Now let's review each and every one of those sections, including the name and the conclusion.

1) Name of the Company — At the top of the first page you will write the name of the company. If you don't have a name yet or if you don't like yours, it is not a problem (yet) as this is not the most important piece of information on this first page. If your business is already active and has a website attached to it, you will also put the URL of the website there.

> **Example**
>
> MyPrivateCoach
> myPrivateCoach.com

2) Mission — Right under the name of your company you are going to state your mission. This is what I call the attention-grabber. This will arouse, or not, an investor's or partner's interest from the beginning. You can also name this Vision depending on how you feel about your business and if there is a very important visionary aspect to it.

The mission statement should not exceed two lines. It shows the level of your ambition, which is essential for your business success.

If you are writing your business plan just for yourself or if you are just thinking about a soft venture, consider the mission statement as the essence of your business. If you cannot summarize it in two sentences, there is something wrong! You should be able to fix this problem by going through each of the remaining sections.

> **Examples**
> - MyPrivateCoach's mission is to become the #1 worldwide reference for all coaching needs.
> - MyPrivateCoach's mission is to become the household name for coaching that includes: life, business, health and fitness, etc.
> - IntelliSystems' mission is to become the #1 worldwide reference online provider for bug management and customer support systems.
> - SuperCom wants to revolutionize the delivery of broadband services by providing a bundled service of telephone, cable and broadband Internet access as one utility service for less than $100 a month.

It is important to have the mission of the company isolated from the rest of the plan, as it forces the writer to really take the time to think about the core meaning of the business. Because this sentence is not buried under a lot of surrounding text, it has to be right to the point to be powerful.

3) Executive Summary

Though the Executive Summary stands on the first page of your business plan, you will write it at the end. Indeed, only when you have thoroughly gone through all the sections will you have an in-depth understanding of your venture. This will allow you to write a concise, powerful, and appealing summary.

This section will not extend beyond the first page. It will cover all of the following areas excluding your conclusion: company description, the products or services you intend to produce and sell, how you plan to do so, who will be in charge. You will finish with a short phrase on your financials. If you are looking for venture capital, this last sentence is the key for your reader. This is where you will state how much you are looking for and why. It will read like, "We are looking to raise $2 million dollars to support our international growth, hire a new VP of Sales, and engage a marketing campaign."

4) Company Description

We are now at the top of the second page of your business plan. Now that we know the name of your company and its mission, we need to present what this business is about. This overview will cover the following:

- A short industry briefing
- Corporate history if applicable (how long has this company been in existence, past history, etc.)
- The legal structure

If you already have shareholders (apart from you), and if you've already had a round of funding, this is the place to talk about it.

5) Products and/or Service

This is the "meat" of this document. After all, this is the reason why you are writing this business plan in the first place. Obviously, you want to produce "something." You want to generate value, whether by creating a new killer technology, publishing a new type of step-by-step books, comparing prices on the Internet, or by re-inventing coaching, for instance.

This section features the following:

Description of the products/services. You will need to be very specific. However, do not include more than one or two charts in this part. Additional information like blueprints, detailed explanations, and pictures should go in the appendix section.

Research and development. You will also describe this process, and if the progress is pertinent. If you have patented findings, state this here as well. Note that you will also show it in your financials when you present an evaluation for your patents.

Pricing. You can also brush on this but not about the business model in this section.

Delivery. A critical part is how you plan to deliver the product or service to your clients, and why you chose this approach.

> **Examples**
> - **Description**: "Company XYZ will produce Super-Ink cartridges that offer 200% more printing capacity. Thanks to a patent pending solution (#78HJ768J) XYZ can address 90% of the printers on the market. Refer to Appendix 4C for detailed blueprints of Super-Ink cartridges."
> - **Delivery**: "Intellibug will be delivered to small and mid-size software companies in an ASP model only. We do not plan on providing enterprise solutions for cost reasons. ASP will allow us to grow our market share rapidly, and to upgrade and fix bugs without having to put in place heavy logistics. An ASP approach also allows us to apply the "pizza price solution" described in our Marketing and Sales Section."

Of course this presentation should be longer, and explain in more details how the products and services work, what their strong and weak points are. However, though it is essential to know your weak points, you do not want to feature them too blatantly.

Target two pages for this section unless your product is highly technical, requiring lengthy explanations. In that case you are "permitted" to go to up to ten pages.

If you feel you can cover this section in less than two pages, by all means limit yourself to the most concise text possible.

6) Marketing and Sales

Even if you are not looking for funding, you really need to spend time on this section.

Why? Because we are back to the "let's force ourselves" to think about what we really want to do.

You will first start by defining your market. If you need to have focus groups or if you ran some polls, indicate it here. These methods of gathering market data are highly regarded by potential investors, so make sure to do your homework when analyzing the market. You need to go further than just writing, "I think that this market would like my product because I like it." This is nice, of course, but not sufficient!

This market definition needs to have numbers in it. You need to quantify the market, its size, its geographical location, its history if relevant, and provide other demographics if necessary.

Examples
- "61 million American adults, or 57% of those with Internet access, have used the Web to get health or medical information...more than 50% have used the Web for shopping (47%) stock quotes (44%), or sports scores (36%)." (Pew Internet & American Life Project)
- "51% of physicians look for drug information on the Internet" (AMA)
- "Based on our latest research (in partnership with Accenture Consulting), we have established that the potential size of our target market would be 150 million people in the USA alone. A reasonable worldwide target for ISB Systems would be a 5% market share, hence, 7.5 million potential clients."

Again, this is too short to reflect an actual section, but it is a good example that you can expand on.

A good source for free marketing information is MarketingSherpa.com. If you have cash to spend on serious marketing studies, go for the Gartner Group Reports. They are a good alternative to an expensive market consultant. Another option is to get access to the Harvard Business Review.

Examples
The November 2004 issue of the Harvard Business Review has an article entitled The Wild West of Executive Coaching. In that article it states "Annual spending on coaching is estimated at roughly $1 billion."

Numbers coming from a highly respected source always carry a lot of weight. Take the time you need to gather relevant and verified (very important) data.

Now that you have defined the market, you need to characterize your customer. Gender, income level, age group and ethnicity are usually relevant. Again, you need to support these claims with the appropriate research.

Once these two elements have been defined, you want to write a paragraph on your competition. Here, distinguish between direct and indirect competition.

How do you define direct and indirect? Direct is somebody doing the exact same thing as you. For instance, if you want to develop a spreadsheet then, Excel and Lotus would be direct competitors.

Indirect competition has more to do with ways used by people to achieve the desired result or solve the burning need but in an ineffective way. For instance, if you want to sell a software bug-tracking system, then an Excel spreadsheet could be your indirect competition. It is less effective, it takes longer, queries are limited, etc., but they are currently in use satisfying a market need.

It is useful to show you did your homework on this part, but make sure you paint a competitive picture which is not too frightening. You should not have to put more weight on the negative part of your plan than on the positive part. However, if you feel at one point that the picture is "grim," you may have to go back to the drawing board and re-think: Are you in the right market? Do you have what it takes to address such fierce competition? Do you have the right partners and experience?

I strongly suggest you do a SWOT analysis. SWOT stands for: **S**trengths, **W**eaknesses, **O**pportunities and **T**hreats.

A SWOT looks like this:

NOTE Please use the template available at http://HappyAbout.info/jointventuring/

Strengths	Weaknesses	Opportunities	Threats
Strength 1	Weakness 1	Opportunity 1	Threat 1
Strength 2	Weakness 2	Opportunity 2	Threat 2
Strenth n	Weakness n	Opportunity n	Threat n

This is a straightforward document, which is very helpful and which allows busy investors to get an instant picture of your situation. If your list of Weaknesses and Threats is longer than Strengths and Opportunities, it is time to stop and reflect upon this result. Take action! Find out if you can "fight" against those odds or not.

You have defined the market, your target customer base and your competition. It is now time to present your winning strategy. This is where you need to shine.

Be creative! Show what will make you (and the partner or investor) a winner. Why will you be better than the others? Will you deliver faster, cheaper, newer, etc.? Describe all of this.

> **Example**
> - We want to apply the same sales strategy that has proven to be successful at our current company: demonstrating to prospects that we can do at least as well, or better, as an in-house solution, but at a significant fraction of the cost (ten times lower).
> - Pizza style pricing strategy
> - Though we haven't finalized our pricing strategy, the use of our services will be subscription based. Additionally, due to the high customization level of our system, we foresee several levels of pricing based on the features that customers are willing to pay for ('toppings'). To have the broadest possible market coverage, both the bug management and support systems will be available in many different versions ranging from a non-customizable basic setup (cheaper), to a fully customizable "look and feel" and kernel features (more expensive). Of course, the pricing will also involve the number of users, projects and/or supported products. Note: A pricing system that is too complicated might be counter-productive for closing sales. For example, start-ups may be looking for a fast and affordable way to get a bug management system, while Fortune 500 companies may be ready to go for the high end of the pricing spectrum. In this regard, two different facades (web sites), based on the same infrastructure, each appealing to one of these two distinct market segments, will be beneficial.

We are planning on implementing the following three distribution channels:

1. Online Sales – Allowing small companies to order, pay for and install our solution as fast as possible. Online payment guarantees

immediate fee collection hence a stable and recurrent cash flow. A very limited sales force will be required. Targets include: USA, Asia and Europe.

2. IT Consulting Partnerships – This will allow us to expand our market without having to invest in a top-notch sales team. For example, since the culture of buying software online has not been fully developed in Europe, this approach will guarantee we penetrate the market quickly. Note: We have already established a relationship with the #1 IT Consulting Firm in Spain and a large French IT consulting firm (SSII).

3. Affiliate Sales – These will expand our exposure at no cost and will have the same advantages as online sales.

To validate our concept, we are talking to local start-ups and are in the process of securing three LOIs for use of our beta version.

In this section, you will want to present your promotion strategy, i.e. how you will market your product or your services. Venues could be:

- Direct marketing via E-mail
- Direct mail
- Telemarketing
- Sponsoring events
- Hiring a public relations firm to get the word out
- Writing articles and distributing them
- Special offers
- Partnerships
- Motivating your affiliates

If you already have partnerships, events, or a promotion strategy in place, describe how this will evolve and why you are fine-tuning it.

Always try to use the word "fine-tune" instead of "change" or "dramatically change," etc., as this can raise red flags in an investor's or partner's mind.

7) Operations

You will find this section named "Execution" in some books about how to write a business plan. It does not matter because both titles cover the same ground. This is where you will present elements like:

- **Legal and government issues**: Are there any regulations that can have an effect on your business?
- **Staffing**: Show how you plan on ramping up, the positions you will need to fill, who is already on board, and how you plan on finding your new employees (online tools, recruiting firms, etc.)
- **Suppliers**: List the types of suppliers you plan to deal with, where they are located, whether you need special authorization to interact with specific suppliers, whether you have a past track record with them.
- **Alliances**. Depending on the market you are targeting, you may need to enter alliances to penetrate the market much faster and much more efficiently. Describe why and how you intend to partner with specific people, companies or organizations. Define the respective level of involvement, the required investment, if any, and how much discussion has already been conducted.

- **Policies**. Succinctly present the specific policies you will have to implement for your business to exist.
- **Risk assessment**. There is always risk involved when one starts a business, be it a full-scale venture or a soft one. Being able to assess the level of risk is very important and can make the difference between a successful launch or an endeavor fraught with lawsuits, accidents, marketing errors, and more.
- **Facilities and location**. Where will you work? If you plan on having employees, describe where they will be working. If you are creating an actual object, explain where it will be produced and how it will be shipped from one place to another. Depict how the facilities function, how they interact with one another (if relevant), and how they fit in your general business flow. If you plan on having several facilities this is where you will explain what each of them will do.
- **Insurance**. Each business needs to be covered with business insurance. Liability, loss, damage, etc. are all forms of viable insurance. Briefly present which types of insurance you need, and if you have to purchase industry specific insurance plans. Explain why and how much this will cost. Assessing your risks seriously will help you determine the type of insurance you need to purchase.
- **Milestones in your development**. Show your roadmap, and indicate your major milestones. What happens if you don't reach a key milestone? If you plan on manufacturing a tangible product, explain when it will be ready to hit the market. Partners, investors, bankers and solopreneurs need to have a realistic

roadmap. This is another type of indispensable document a businessperson cannot live without.

8) Management

As its title indicates, this section will list key job descriptions, responsibilities, management team, organizational chart, and advisors, if any.

The management team is critical to a solid business plan. If you don't yet have the funds to attract the talent you need, you can still find your staff with a future promise to come aboard when funding is complete. In this case, list your team members' "acting titles" (example: Acting VP of Sales). To strengthen the human factor, it is strongly suggested that you assemble a board of advisors to add further credibility to your business. In a full-scale venture, this implies talking experts in your field into becoming helpful counselors: business, strategy, industry, marketing, etc.

If you are in a solo-entrepreneur type of business and you are writing this business plan for yourself, then this section does not have to be as comprehensive as the others. This means that you don't have to spend a tremendous amount of time on this part. The exception to this is if you have the desire to grow from a personnel standpoint. If you do, make sure you think about what profiles would most help you develop your company.

For soft ventures, take the time to think about your unofficial advisory board. Having experts around you will help you reach your goals faster. If your project is interesting, you will be sure to find successful businessmen and women ready to lend a hand and make your project a winner.

If you have a team or promises from people to come on board once you have the funding, make sure to briefly describe their relevant experience, their credentials in the field, and any publications they have made and in general. Anything that can make your people shine will make this management team even more of a winner in the eyes of your investor.

> **Example**
>
> **Steven Banks, President**
> Steven Banks is the President of SuperStoreonLine. Steven is also the President and owner of SSL Facilities, a key distribution partner of SuperStoreonLine.
>
> - His expertise in on-line stores development along with over 22 years of consumer products distribution experience, and 10 years as COO of AmazoniaRiver.com (listed on the NASDAQ: AMRR), are valuable assets to SuperStoreonLine. Steven holds a BA from Stanford University and an MBA from Louisiana State University.

9) Financials

Working on financial projections, knowing how you will use the funds you may raise, and finding out when you will break even is the last decisive element of a business plan. In this section you will need the following documents:

- **Profit and Loss**. This is also called an Income Statement. It shows the results of business operations over a period of time (a month, a quarter, half a year or a full year). You can generate this statement for a soft or

full-scale venture. This will serve as your success-rating tool. It will "show" how well you are doing, if you have good margins, and if your product or service is selling well.
- **Balance Sheet**. This is a snapshot of the financial conditions of your company (whether small or big; it doesn't matter, you need one).
- **Cash Flow Statement**. The amount of cash your company generates and uses during a period. It is calculated by adding non-cash charges (such as depreciation) to the net income after taxes. You will use cash flow as an indication of your venture's financial strength.
- **Debt Schedule and Financing**. If your joint venture requires your going into debt to finance your growth, then you will need to show how you will repay this debt on a "debt schedule."
- **Use of Funds**. For full-scale ventures where investors funnel in funds, you will need to explain how those funds will be used and how quick your resources may dry up.
- **Break-Even Analysis**. This is important for any venture, whether soft or full-scale, as it will allow you to understand if you have a chance to recoup your personal investment (time and money), and when. The sooner you break even, the better.
- **Exit Strategy**. Applies to companies funded by venture capitalists. Here you will show when and how you plan to exit (going IPO or being acquired).

To really write an in-depth meaningful Financial Section, you will need the help of a CPA or a Financial Advisor. This will not be necessary for soft ventures, where you only need to have a high-level understanding of how much profit you will generate and in what period of time.

10) Conclusion

Your conclusion should be a very short paragraph. Indeed, no need to summarize your business plan here since you already have an executive summary at the beginning of your document.

Repeating your mission, why you are seeking funding (if you are indeed looking for additional funds) and thanking the reader for taking the time to understand your business model and your concept will do it.

Make sure your last sentence is an aggressive punch line like: "In 2010 the world will wonder how it could improve itself before without MyPrivateCoach!"

Finishing up with an ambitious message can only serve your purpose (self-motivation for yourself and your team as well as leaving a good impression to the reader).

Chapter 4 Highlights

- A business plan is a document that presents the who, what, where, when, why and how of a venture. Your document should cover the following: Mission, Executive Summary, Company Description, Presentation of Products and/or Services, Marketing and Sales, Operations, Management and Financials.
- The "softer" your joint venture, the lighter your business plan will be.
- For full-scale business plans, you may need the help of experts in your industry, marketing information, and accounting expertise.
- You can find examples for each section mentioned or specific documents online by searching for the various templates.
- Have outsiders (entrepreneurs) read your business plan as you go forward. This will allow you to see if all the information you presented is clear enough and flows easily for the reader.

- Your homework is thus to start working on your business flight plan right now and let it take form as you go through this book.

chapter 5
Human Resources and Skills Integration

Brian Tracy, best-selling author of motivational books

"Teamwork is so important that it is virtually impossible for you to reach the heights of your capabilities or make the money that you want without becoming very good at it."

The size of your business could range anywhere from two people to a few dozen. Hence, in this chapter you will find key tips and tricks on how to tackle the human factor: how to rapidly assess skills, share knowledge, empower your teams and move forward as fast as you can. Indeed, I believe that it is not the big shark that swallows the small fish, but the fast shark that eats the slow fish. Speed is a key success determinant.

As you handle the human factor to the best of your ability, you will pave your joint venture's way to success. This implies translating your business plan into people terms and developing a high level of trust between the players of your joint venture. Ultimately, you will create a hybrid culture that will possess the top practices and skill sets from each side. It is best in this process to clearly identify respective weaknesses, to avoid transferring them from one side to the other.

Bear in mind that depending on the type of partnership you are entering, all the sections of this chapter may not be relevant to your situation. I suggest, however, that you read them as they may motivate you to think in broader terms and develop your joint venture beyond your original objective.

There are seven areas you need to consider:

- **Assessing** and **recording** skills
- **Managing** skill gaps
- **Leveraging** organization resources
- **Coaching** employees or partners in knowledge transfer
- **Building** and **empowering** teams
- **Attracting** new talent and retaining your employees
- **Protecting** the people in your venture

Assessing and recording skills

Now that you have engaged your venture, selected the right partner, and finalized your business plan, you need to conduct an in-depth assessment of the resources at hand. You will have to determine the specific competencies that will make your joint venture successful, and identify those thought patterns and work ethics which may undermine your efforts.

Assessing and recording your people's skills, including yours, is now your priority. You will look at both hard skills and soft skills.

Hard skills refer to technical abilities acquired for a specific job or function, i.e industry-specific core competencies or position-specific know-how.

Soft skills are interpersonal skills such as knowing how to communicate successfully, being able to manage time efficiently, having the ability to handle and manage change effectively, mastering conflict resolution techniques, and being a good networker.

Depending on the position you are recording soft skills for, you may add knowing how to balance work and personal life, the ability to encourage teamwork, the ability to collaborate, and being result-oriented.

In times of uncertainty, such as when two businesses enter a strategic alliance, it is important to identify the key indicators of leaders who can manage change seamlessly: networking ability, past successful transitions, and proven understanding of changing business objectives.

The output of your work could look like the following graph, where grey columns represent requisite skills. As you can see from this example, Hard Skill 1 is a necessary skill which is not covered by your present resources. This is what I call a skill gap.

NOTE Please use the template available at http://HappyAbout.info/jointventuring/

	Soft Skil 1	Soft Skil 2	Hard Skill 1	Hard Skill 2	Hard Skill 3
Mitchell	X	X		X	
Valerie	X	X			X
Baptiste		X		X	
Natasha				X	
Eli		X			
Mariah					X
Chen					
Muni				X	X

To better understand how to define the skill sets you are listing, you can use resources like Hewitt.com and the website of the Society for Human Resources Management (http://www.shrm.org).

Homework

- List the key skills (hard and soft) you have determined to be critical for your business objectives.
- List the thought patterns and work ethics you want to avoid at all costs.
- Rank the skills in a descending order of importance.
- Interview all the key players in the joint venture, and assess and list their main skills.
- Match recorded skills with required skills to determine if you have a skills gap.
- Identify your leaders.

Managing skill gaps

You know what you want to find in the people involved in your joint venture. You have interviewed all the key players and assessed their hard and soft skills. You have matched them up with your list of requirements.

In some instances you will be lucky enough to cover all the ground. There may be situations where you will have skill gaps, i.e. one or more key skills are missing: hard (a new position-specific competency) or soft (nobody has ever experienced a successful transition to a joint venture). In this case you will need to close the skill gaps and go over this hurdle by:

- Hiring consultants and coaches (mainly for missing soft skills)
- Applying new human capital strategies to use your existing resources and learn how to be successful without the missing skill
- Attracting new talents who possess the missing competency
- Training existing players
- Bringing in another partner if a major skill is missing. Be careful that this key missing skill is not an indicator that you did not do your homework well before launching your joint venture
- Contacting successful joint venturers you know and asking for their opinion and support

Your Homework

- Decide if your best course of action (time and money-wise) is not to learn how to live without this skill.
- Identify ways to go over the skill gap hurdle.
- Implement the desired course of action.

Important Facts

- Starting a joint venture may be stressful at times. It is important that you do not let a skill gap destabilize your self-confidence, or worse, stop you. Do not procrastinate. Take care of it as soon as you have identified this stumbling block. The most important factor is to never keep any energy drainer on your mind.
- Discovering a critical skill gap may be a sign you did not sufficiently study all the facets of your joint venture. You may want to go back to the drawing board and reconsider who is bringing what, when, why and how to the party.

Leveraging organization resources

You don't need to re-invent the wheel. Too often we think that we need to start from scratch and re-invent processes, methods or policies when they are here. They may be well hidden sometimes, but still they exist and finding them will help save your time.

You need to first identify which processes need to be put in place to support the business goals, and hence the organizational objectives, of your joint venture.

This is one step higher than the skill assessment and recording. Here you want to assess, record, and use the existing processes. Leveraging your venture resources will definitely propel you towards your goal faster than expected.

Evaluate the following:

- HR processes
- Leadership processes
- Delegation level
- Existence of a community of practice
- Are there any training programs in place?
- Do you and your partners have access to large and/or specific networks?
- Are administrative processes identical? If yes, the integration is straightforward; if not, then evaluate the most well-organized one and get rid of the inefficient one

To do these things, you will need to interview the key players in the venture as well as some entry-level people who can share their knowledge of "buried" procedures with you. In large corporations, you may find catalogs of procedures that allow human resources to be dealt with in a very efficient manner. In smaller organizations or in coalescent joint ventures, you will not find such organized documents. While you do not want to waste your time writing and filling binders with processes and procedures, you will soon realize that having processes clearly outlined in an easily accessible format will make your life easier. And in the joint venture world, having well-defined tasks means you will reach success faster!

> **Homework**
> - List your required processes (in generic terms)
> - Match them with the existing organizational processes
> - Eliminate unnecessary and redundant procedures
> - Inform all participants in the joint venture of all new, crossed-out, or modified processes as a procedure is of no use if nobody knows about it

Coaching employees or partners in knowledge transfer

Knowledge transfer between the joint venture players will enhance the overall skills of your organization and speed up your business expansion. However this apparently simple process is not always as easy as it seems.

Barriers to knowledge transfer may be:

- Panic of the unknown
- Jealousy
- Apprehension of loss of power
- Fear of being replaced
- Lack of time in a very tense environment
- Absence of knowledge transfer process
- Lack of confidence
- Fear of speaking to a group
- Lack of recognition

One of the best-proven ways to flatten these stumble blocks is to use coaching, consulting, or other supporting and motivating techniques.

> **Homework**
> - Have a business coach interview all key players in one-on-one sessions to identify psychological blocks
> - Depending on the difficulties:
>   - Set up public speaking training sessions for shy managers
>   - Increase the level of recognition
>   - Put training sessions in place
>   - Comfort middle and top managers in their positions
>   - Provide more information by better communicating the joint venture objectives, the way events are going to unfold, and the whole gamut of potentialities this joint venture represents

Building and empowering teams

A joint venture cannot exist if there is only one person involved. The essence of such a strategic alliance is that a team is formed around a particular goal, for a specific duration, and with people offering complementary skill sets.

Margaret Mead

"Never doubt that a small group of thoughtful, committed people can change the world; indeed, it is the only thing that ever has."

Michael Jordan | **"Talent wins games, but teamwork and intelligence win championships."**

Whatever the size of your team, you will need to make it aware of its status of team to greatly increase performance levels. But let's first define the concept of a team and answer generic questions about this subject:

- What makes a person part of team
- What "being part of a team" means
- What the purpose of the team is
- What the team's dynamics are

We may all have different answers for these questions; however you need to answer yes to all of the following questions to guarantee your team is at its optimum level. Questions to which you answer no will be your next job: deal with them right away, whichever they might be because there is nothing worse than an unmotivated team!

> **Homework**
>
> - Ask yourself the following questions (you can use a consultant/coach to interview your team and better understand how it stands):
>   - Is there a well-defined challenge which bonds all the team members?
>   - Is there an obvious team spirit?
>   - Is there a growth potential?
>   - Is there a motivating leader in place?
>   - Is there enough empowerment?
>   - Is there clear feedback on actions?
>   - Are there unambiguous milestones with which team members can identify themselves?
>   - Does the team leader spend quality time with the team members?
>   - Does the team leader shows she cares about her team?
>   - Are there special group events to increase the connection between team members?
>
> - Work on each question for which your answer is no, so that the next time you run through this list, you answer yes to all the questions.

One excellent way to increase the level of efficiency of a team is to empower it. Empowerment does not mean democracy, where all can decide on everything. Rather, it means giving more power to individual contributors. This power is aligned with their skill sets and will allow them to do whatever they deem necessary to reach their goals. Empowerment should not be considered as a useless buzzword concept, as this approach has clearly been shown to seriously increase performance levels among cross-cultural teams.

You can have a "happy about working with you" team if you stay away from the things that can wreak havoc with the team spirit:

- Ruling like a king
- Not caring about the team members
- Not solving conflict in a timely manner
- Absence of communication
- Lack of focus
- Asking for too much
- Lack of accountability
- Not knowing who contributes what and who fits where

Attracting new talent and retaining your employees

If you have identified skill gaps which you need to cover, attracting new talent is one of your main concerns.

Though there are several ways to hire new employees or find additional partners, if you want to spare your hard-earned cash online services may be your best bet: try online job recruiting systems for employees and online high-end networking programs for partners. Look into another book by my publisher called "Happy About LinkedIn for Recruiting" for a roadmap for recruiting within the LinkedIn social network.

Homework

- Define your needs and write job descriptions. They will need to be well done to limit the amount of potential candidates you have to go through. Our favorite new comer in the online recruiting field is Streamjobs.net, which uses a peer-to-peer approach with a deep semantic analysis and ranking of resumes and profiles. You can also work with more-established companies like Monster or YahooJobs.
- Learn the best ways to conduct personal assessments and interviews. Check out this great resource with over 2,000 questions to ask your candidates: www.hr-guide.com/selection.htm
- Create an attractive package for your new talents: challenging job, stock
- options, motivating salary, great growth prospect, incentives tied to the JV success, etc.
- Scout online networks for potential additional partners if needed.

Successfully attracting new talent is one thing, retaining your newly found gem is another. Creating a retention program should be an essential step in your human resource management agenda. Losing human resources is extremely costly to organizations, large or small. Contrary to common belief, it costs less to keep employees and partners happy than to be too cheap and having to constantly look for and interview potential candidates.

Depending on the size of your joint venture, you and your partner can either develop your retention program just by yourselves or with your HR manager and with some other key players in the organization.

Retaining employees implies a competitive compensation, empowerment, supporting creativity, providing growth opportunities, flexibility, respect, knowing them and understanding their needs, organizing bonding activities, and keeping them healthy and happy. **In essence, a good retention program is one that makes people want to wake up and work toward the success of the joint venture.**

Andrew Carnegie, successful entrepreneur and philanthropist

"Teamwork is the ability to work together toward a common vision. The ability to direct individual accomplishments toward organizational objectives. It is the fuel that allows common people to attain uncommon results." -

Protecting the people in your venture

Bringing new talents onboard implies documenting their interview processes, their compensation, their rights, and their expected contributions. Several laws protect employees from being taken advantage of or discriminated against. You must know those laws to avoid a legal faux-pas when interviewing and making an offer. A lawyer is a great friend in this business. I recommend that you spend a few hundred dollars to retain an employment law attorney in your state, so that you can take all appropriate actions to protect your business and your employees.

> **Important Facts**
> - Though your contract can cover all employees' and employer's rights and responsibilities, state and federal laws may dictate other, or different, rights and duties of the different parties.
> - You must be aware of the basic laws like: Title VII, Americans With Disabilities Act (ADA), Age in Discrimination Employment Act, Fair Labor Standards Act, Family and Medical Leave Act, etc.
> - All employees are entitled to the right to privacy and to be free from harassment and discrimination. This applies to partners as well.

The things you should keep in mind:

- No religious, race, nationality, gender, age, or physical capacity discrimination should ever be conducted.
- Document all interviews and justify rejection of candidates in official letters. E-mails and phone conversations are not enough.
- Sign a detailed contract with newcomers and with transferred employees in the cases of large joint ventures: who will do what, specific milestones, etc.

One of our favorite online resources for Human Resource Management legal issues is FindLaw.com – Small Business. Here you can find a wealth of legal information pertaining to employment as well as find local lawyers. A great book in this field is Everyday Employment Law: The Basics, by Amy DelPo and Lisa Guerin (Nolo).

In addition to the legal counsel you may receive from qualified attorneys, there are a few tips you can apply to your daily management to avoid legal troubles with employees:

- **Communication**: have an open door policy. It will show you care about the workplace, and it will help inform you early on of problems that could potentially lead to legal troubles.
- **Equality**: treat all joint venture players equally. Don't play favorites; apply the same performance standards to all. When assessing the members of a team, use the same guidelines. Regularity in your evaluation is also a key factor of legal protection.
- **Respect**: when an employee or a partner shares personal problems with you, do not repeat them to the team. Keep your lips closed tightly. Not only will you show respect for your teammate, but you will also protect yourself against accusations of defamation and emotional distress.
- **Never, ever discriminate**: all your decisions are to be based on business facts, and not on intangible aspects like race, faith, age or gender.
- **Employee handbook**: if your company is large enough (i.e. not limited to two partners), take the time to write an employee handbook. It does not have to be too time-consuming, as there are several templates available online. Just type "template employee handbook" into a search engine and you will find great resources. Always have your output validated by an employment law attorney.

- **Take action**: when there is a problem, don't wait and pray for it to get resolved by itself. Don't let a small trouble turn into a major mess.

Chapter 5 Highlights

- To get a better grip on your human resources you will need to conduct a thorough **skill assessment**.
- You may identify a **skill gap** which you will need to take care of quickly: either by learning how to live without this particular skill or by bringing this skill in-house.
- Bringing people from different horizons into a joint venture requires a **hybrid culture** and a true **team spirit**. Once this is established, **knowledge transfer** will become easier and goals will be achieved faster.
- **Procedures** are indispensable to all businesses, small and large. Before starting to re-invent the wheel, verify that you don't already have all needed procedures in place. Eliminate redundant ones.
- Make sure your business and your employees are **legally protected** by spending time with an employment law attorney. Draft all necessary documents and submit them for professional review.

Chapter 6
Plan Execution

Marshal Ferdinand Foch

"The fundamental qualities for good execution of a plan is first; intelligence; then discernment and judgment, which enable one to recognize the best method as to attain it; the singleness of purpose; and, lastly, what is most essential of all, will, stubborn will."

Planning is an important success factor. However, it is simply not enough. Execution is essential. I like to say that once you are done with planning, the easiest and most boring part of starting a joint venture is behind you. Now the heart-lifting feeling of working towards tangible success will be your companion for the weeks and months to come.

You now are equipped with your bible: the joint venture business plan. You have identified your ideal partner, and you have the required funds to, at least, get started.

The next step is simply to turn your words into actions, your forecasts into results and your dreams into reality.

To do so successfully, you will need a no-fail process, which I will call The Ultimate Plan Execution System™.

You will need to work on the following six elements:

- **Execution plan**
- **Time management**
- **Organization**
- **Communication**
- **Handling frustration**
- **Staying healthy**

As you can see from this list, the human factor is back in our priority list, as you need to maintain your body and your mind in a can-do attitude at all times. This requires building a supportive environment as well as taking care of yourself from a health perspective. How often do we hear entrepreneurs working twenty hours a day, going two days without sleep, not having the time to exercise, go for a short walk around the block or eating healthy meals? You and your partners are the backbone of your venture. You need to be kept intact.

Execution Plan

How much of your venture project do you clearly see? You might think you have a very clear picture of what it is about and what the outcome should be, but try to dive in at a lower level and your project might seem a little fuzzy around the edges. Do not fret over this unclear perspective, as it is customary for entrepreneurs to want to stay at a macro-level vision.

Business plans usually contain an execution plan as potential partners, investors, lenders or employees need to have a clear vision as far as what needs to be done. However, if you extract your execution plan from your business plan and look at it, you will see that it is not detailed enough; the purpose of a business plan is not to overwhelm readers with thousands of small actions.

Your work will now consist in creating a master execution plan with intermediary milestones. You will go over each step listed in the plan and expand it. Use a spreadsheet or a project management tool like Microsoft Project, for example. Remember, project management consists of handling time, resources, money and scope at the same time, and often on the same document. It is a tricky exercise like writing a business plan, but more rewarding because it offers a clear vision as to how fast you are moving towards your success.

> **Homework**
>
> - Break down your project (the joint venture launch and growth) into large categories. For example: Fund raising, product development, human resources, etc.
> - Develop each component into sub-categories for as many levels as required by your plan.
> - When you have reached the lowest level of sub-categories, list the tasks to be performed.
> - List your resources: internal and already committed resources as well as external resources (consultants, coaches and advisors).
> - Link each task to at least one resource and add a completion date.
> - Determine the task dependencies and order your tasks accordingly.
> - Try as much as possible to put your tasks in parallel order to save precious time.
> - Determine the critical path for your overall project.

You will need to determine who is in charge of managing the project.

Who will:

- Update the schedule
- Push resources so that deadlines are met
- Modify tasks and reporting

There can only be one person responsible for managing the master plan; otherwise the absence of a clear direction may lead to failure. In small joint ventures, usually one partner in particular who is chosen for his or her ability to stick to a plan, motivate the troops, and in general, get things done. In larger companies, you may hire a project manager whose sole responsibility will be to execute the plan and coordinate resources.

> **Important Facts**
>
> Though it is critical to manage your project and be detail-oriented, be careful not to use up too much time on this task, which should only support your executing the plan and not swallow up the bulk of your resources.

Time Management

Run a poll in a startup or large corporation and ask what is most frustrating about the company in general, what could be improved, and you will invariably get the same answer at the top of the list: "Lack of time."

As a venturer, you have dozens of tasks to handle. Meeting with investors and partners, developing a product, finding the best resources at the best price, market your product, develop your supporting structure, and handle day-to-day administrative activities are just some of them. You may feel that you are juggling too many obligations over the course of a day. At the same time, do you ever feel amazed at how some people seem to accomplish so much in the exact same amount of time allotted to us all? Since your best ally in this business adventure is time, we will learn to "create" enough time to get everything done.

Just as the fundamental key to becoming wealthy is proper money management (managing your earnings, saving, investing and spending), the key to succeeding in accomplishing the ambitious goals you have set for your venture is effective time management.

Recently, reporter John Stossel of ABC's 20/20 television news magazine exploded the myth that Americans have less free time now than previous generations did. Once he learned how to manage his time better, he found he was able to write a book, Give Me a Break: How I Exposed Hucksters, Cheats and Scam Artists and Became the Scourge of the Liberal Media....

Surprisingly enough, however, perhaps the most important reason for learning to manage time more effectively is to safeguard one's health. Studies have shown that the frustration engendered by the difficulties in coping with our many daily interruptions- telephone calls, E-mails, unexpected visitors, unplanned meetings, sudden emergencies, etc. -leads to increased levels of stress. The effects of this stress can be gastric and digestive distress, as well as intense fatigue and exhaustion.

Moreover, brain research has found that stress-related fatigue is linked more frequently to anxiety about not having completed what we wanted to complete than to the acute form of stress generated by crises that occasionally come up; hence, the supreme importance of time management.

Managing Communications

You can cut down the amount of time wasted on the telephone by avoiding being placed on hold. If someone is unavailable right away, find out the best time to call back, or leave your number. If you need to make regular calls, try to schedule them in advance according to mutually agreed times.

If a receptionist, secretary or assistant answers your incoming calls, train them to screen calls and refer them to others. Have your staff take messages for you when you do not want to be disturbed, and try to delegate returning some of the phone calls to others.

If you take the call, let the caller know your time constraints. Always keep a pen and pad by the phone. If you get a call asking for information you don't have immediately on hand, don't look for it; arrange to call back later.

You can reduce cell phone interruptions by not giving the number out to too many people, and not including it on your business card or E-mail signature unless it really is too difficult to reach you by other means.

Avoid taking business calls on your car phone. Any time you think you are saving by driving and talking at the same time will evaporate if you become distracted enough to miss a turn or a highway exit. Even more is lost by having to reconstruct the call later or repeating much of the same conversation because you were unable to take notes during the original call.

Most people keep their E-mail programs open and running all day long and are alerted to incoming messages. In addition, a recent study found that 75% of these people would cease other activity to take care of incoming E-mail. This is highly disruptive and prevents you from being truly efficient. Researchers asked the study group to refrain from handling each incoming E-mail as it arrived; instead, they were allowed to read and answer new E-mails only five times a day. The efficiency level of this group increased by 35%.

Turn off your incoming E-mail alert, therefore, and open your E-mail only at regular intervals. Do not let E-mails dictate what your working days should look like. If you are like me and have a hard time disciplining yourself, then have a desktop where your E-mails arrive and work in a meeting room (or in your living room if you are starting your venture as a home-based business) with a laptop. You will be impressed by how much more you get done!

Managing Meetings and Visitors

It is widely acknowledged that about one-third of the time spent in meetings is wasted due to poor meeting management and lack of planning. Reliable estimates indicate that the average executive spends about seventeen hours a week in meetings, about six hours in planning time, and untold hours in follow-up.

One senior executive I know recalls being summoned to meetings every single day of the business week. One meeting per week was labeled product marketing. Another was called strategy, then product testing, then customer review. In addition, one of the five weekly meetings had no fixed agenda. And this does not count ad hoc meetings on issues that might crop up from time to time.

When this executive was not able to convince the CEO to scale back the number of meetings, she decided to work from home 50% of the time; her productivity (measured by closing of contracts) doubled!

It is not necessary to eliminate all meetings, but up to half of internal company meetings might be profitably dispensed with. Take a few minutes to write down how many meetings you attended last week, how many you have planned for the coming week, and how long you think they are going to last. Add up the hours, and slash the number of meetings by two, and/or the number of hours spent in them by 30%.

The same rule for incoming phone calls applies to personal appointments and visitors. If you have a secretary or personal assistant, set a clear policy about who should have access to you and with whom else they might be able to speak.

If you have an unexpected visitor, establish at the start why they have come to see you.

Stand when they enter the room, so that they also remain standing. If it is indeed necessary for you to deal personally with them, suggest a later meeting at your convenience. Set a time limit to your discussion, and avoid engaging in small talk.

If you really can't get them out of your office, make a polite excuse and leave the office yourself.

These tips are by no means exhaustive, but they represent a good start to managing your most precious resource: time.

Important Facts

- Time management is a myth! Whatever you do, you will never have more than twenty-four hours a day. However, by learning how to use those hours more effectively, you will end up achieving more in less time.
- Remember Pareto's principle: 20% of what you do is responsible for 80% of your results.

Organization | Organizing your tasks optimally goes hand in hand with time management.

To significantly ameliorate your organization, you can:

- Learn how to **delegate** better. You know which resources are available, thanks to your work on the business plan. Reassign responsibilities to your partner or to subordinates. Not only will you save precious time, but you will also improve the level of self-confidence of people who work with you.
- **Prioritize** ruthlessly. Keep an up-to-date to-do list, and review it every morning before starting your day. Select your top five tasks of the day. If you do not complete them by the end of the day, ask yourself why, and take all necessary actions to have them completed by the following day.
- **Plan** your days ahead. Always save free time for unexpected tasks, meetings or urgent decisions.
- As much as possible, establish **routines**. Our brain functions much better when it does not have to think "what's next."
- Understand your own **attention span**. Several studies have shown that the **average attention span** is 45 minutes. This varies from one person to another, but keep it as a time limit for your tasks. If your attention span is shorter, then work in 30-minute time blocks.
- **Organize your data**. Filing systems must be well organized and documented. On your desktop, organize your E-mails and files into clearly defined folders. Create rules for all your incoming and outgoing E-mails.

Communication

Whether your venture is composed of two partners or of a larger group of people, always keep in mind that all involved parties want to get feedback on the advancement of the project.

Without becoming sick with "meetingitis," your organization will greatly benefit from a high level of transparency. Inform your team on how well things are progressing. Celebrate your successes. Have small celebrations for intermediary milestones, and extraordinary events for major accomplishments.

This will ensure that you keep a high level of motivation within your group. Being part of celebrations will also bond employees beyond the average connection one can find in a large well-established corporation. It will involve each and every person, and all parties will feel this venture is their "baby" to some extent and they are responsible for its success.

Problems and concerns should be shared as well. Your team is working hard to help you and your partner reach your goals. They deserve to know when the achievements are not aligned with your goals. In small ventures (two partners for instance), the level of transparency can be complete, and everything can be shared. In larger groups, however, you should be careful not to share your problems too easily with your entire team. You are a leader. You know how to handle stress. This may not be the main characteristic of your team. To avoid creating useless panicky reactions, carefully prepare your speech when announcing serious problems.

Encourage vertical and horizontal communications. Your team members should feel free to come and talk with you or with their colleagues.

> **Homework**
> - Schedule weekly meetings with your team. If you need to share major negative events, rehearse your speech beforehand. If you plan on sharing great news, prepare a small celebration (a lunch out, a sporting event, etc.)
> - Make a point of keeping those meetings at almost all costs. Too often we cancel important informative meetings for supposed emergencies that take the place of communicating with our people. By sending out the right message, i.e. communication is important, and I respect your right to know, you will guarantee a high level of commitment and trust from your team.

Handling Frustration

"I am so frustrated!" We have all, at one point or another, pronounced those words or some other more aggressive phrases.

You are an entrepreneur, a risk-taker, and a person who is doing everything possible to get things done. It is natural to feel frustration when things don't go according to plan. You need to find ways to let this frustration out without turning into anger, despair or pessimism. Most importantly, you should never project your frustrations onto your partner(s) or team members.

Try to understand the origins of your frustration or your partner's frustration:

- Is it because you are not going as fast you thought you would?
- Is it because you are losing faith in your project?
- Do you have to face setbacks?
- Is it because some of your partners are not working out as planned?
- Are you lacking sleep, which can prevent you from looking at the situation with the right perspective?
- Are you putting too much pressure on yourself, your team, your partners, and your family?
- Is your perfectionism going too far?

Whatever the reasons are, it is important that all parties in the venture understand how to release frustration and stress, before it turns sour and prevents you from reaching your goals and from making this venture a success.

Ways to discharge negative pressure can be:

- Meditation.
- Jogging or any other aerobic activity.
- Punching a bag.
- Talking to an outsider about the venture. The purpose is to vent and remove this weight from your shoulders
- Taking care of yourself: getting a massage, soaking in a hot tub, getting pampered.

As the leader of the venture, make sure you attach enough importance to your colleagues' feelings and help them surmount those moments of tension. Keeping harmony in the venture is a key factor of success.

Homework

Tackle frustrations as they arise. Do not let them build up and turn into anger. This is a guaranteed path to failure. Keep harmony within the venture.

Staying Healthy

Executing the venture implies that you need to follow your business plan, follow your execution plan, and learn how to use your resources wisely.

This includes your health. Too often I see entrepreneurs and joint venturers failing, close to their goal, through lack of energy, excessive stress, and poor nutrition.

Because health is rarely linked to business success, it is not an obvious success factor when launching and growing a joint venture. However, it is a key component of your success. Treat your body and your mind well, and they will support long hours, stressful times and moments of joy.

Homework

- Get at least seven hours of sound sleep per day. Learn how to de-stress before going to bed. Do not take any work in your bed. Do not watch violent movies right before going to sleep as this may impair your ability to fall asleep. Avoid heavy dinners as well.
- Exercise at least three times a week. Once a day is optimum but not always feasible in the context of a joint venture launch. Aim for a sixty minute walk per day. This can be fractioned into several walks over the course of the day. Try walking for fifteen minutes right when you wake up. This will help you get fresh oxygen in and get your blood flowing as well. During the day, go for short ten-minute walks.
- Try yoga. Even ten minutes a day can do wonders and help remove tensions in the shoulders and lower back.
- Eat a healthy diet. Ten servings of veggies/fruits a day. Start your day with freshly squeezed orange juice. Avoid having pizzas, burritos or hamburgers delivered to your office. This will trigger fatigue attacks in the afternoon when your body needs to use more energy to think about your business plan instead of digesting this rich food!
- Spend time with a group of friends. Go to the movies. Organize small de-stressing parties at home.
- Keep your health in check.
- Most importantly, never over-work yourself! Working eighteen hours a day is not a sustainable situation.

Chapter 6 Highlights

- Never ever let the venture take your sanity over!
- Executing the plan requires the mastering of several easy-to-acquire skills like time management, communication, organization, and body and spirit maintenance.
- Make sure you keep healthy habits right from the beginning. Teach them to your partners and team members. The same applies to time management and organization. By leading by example, you will increase tenfold your chances for success!

Chapter 7

New Brand Marketing

David Ogilvy | *"You now have to decide what 'image' you want for your brand. Image means personality. Products, like people, have personalities, and they can make or break them in the market place."*

In our highly competitive market, a strong brand is an invaluable and fundamental asset in the market share battle; it sends the right message to the right target market.

If you have merged two companies, two product lines, or two programs into one, then you have to work on marketing the joint venture to your combined existing customer bases. *This does not apply if your joint venture is meant to work as a back office or remain a discrete organization.*

You will need to create an effective integrated plan. This involves:

1. Product marketing strategies. Do you need a new trade name, or do you wish to keep the two brands in existence?
2. Your internal resources for marketing the new brand or reinforcing the existing one: marketing, advertising, and publicity.
3. Your Public Relations and Marketing battle plan.

Product Marketing Strategies: Do You Need a New Brand?

If you are joining forces for complementary products or programs, you can:

1. Keep products separated under their respective brands.
2. Keep products separated, but put each with a new brand that will take advantage of your new name and media coverage.
3. Combine your products/programs under a new brand and in a new package/presentation

In the highly competitive global market, companies are confronted with these options. It is very important, critical even; that you take the appropriate time to address these three approaches. In some instances, you can even opt for all of the above-mentioned strategies with:

1. Two existing lines kept with their respective name and pitch.
2. The same products sold under another brand with new packaging. This will help transitioning smoothly to the new brand, should you realize that one brand needs to be "killed."
3. Products sold under their old and new brand and the two products combined into a new package.

This can be your approach if you are short on resources and want to explore all your potential strategies without making a drastic decision upfront.

I recommend *The 22 Immutable Laws of Branding* by Al Ries and Laura Ries (HarperCollins). It is one of the best references in branding. "Marketing is building a brand in the mind of the prospect," they write. "If you can build a powerful brand, you will have a powerful marketing program. If you can't, then all the advertising, fancy packaging, sales promotion and public relations in the world won't help you achieve your objective." They present clear rules such as The Law of Expansion, The Law of Contraction, The Law of Consistency, and The Law of Mortality.

An example of multiple brands is Chanel, the classy cosmetics brand distributed around the world. Their products under the Chanel brand sell for a high price while the same products sold under their Bourgeois brand sell for less than half the price of Chanel's products. The same applies to L'Oreal and Lancôme (Lancôme being the higher-end store brand, L'Oreal being the drugstore brand). They also use the same products for other satellite brands, depending on the countries they are penetrating. However, these companies have very large marketing budgets, so you may not be able to follow in their footsteps, but looking at what others do is always very useful when wondering what your strategy should be.

The counter example to this would be corporations who decide to merge their products into a unique brand. If we stay in the cosmetics arena, Maybelline acquired Gemey in France. For a few months, the two brands were written on beauty products, Gemey – Maybelline. In 2006, you can see that Gemey has ceased to exist in France on certain products, and Maybelline has become the sole brand. This can be your decision if you wish to be known under only one recognized and reputed brand. You will be taking the risk of losing your faithful brand-loving market if you do this. But combining markets has its advantage in terms of marketing costs (materials, press, public relations, etc.).

> **Homework**
> - Evaluate your combined customer bases: how many, who buys what, etc.
> - Conduct a poll to assess brand loyalty and the risk of losing customers should you discontinue one of the brands. Ask for suggestions. Loyal customers love to be part of your success!
> - Evaluate the economic costs of keeping, combining or creating a new brand (or all of the above).
> - Based on those numbers, make a decision and enforce it by communicating heavily, internally and externally.

If you decide that a new name is the key to your joint success, then you will need to carefully plan this transition. Being "as smooth as possible" should be your motto. Avoid confusion at all costs, as confusion means lost sales.

It is important that you plan this name shift very carefully to keep your loyal customers in the process. It is equally critical that you inform your teams about this change, and that you can demonstrate how this change will be beneficial to all parties including you, your teams, the joint venture, and, ultimately, the clients.

In these new brand launches, even the "big guys" make major mistakes. In 1987 Coca-Cola decided to launch a "New Coke" to celebrate their one hundredth anniversary. Although they spent over $4 million in advertising campaigns, this was a major failure. Why? Because the corporation spent more time strategizing on marketing models at a higher level and applying book-concepts, rather than listening to the main factor in its business: the end consumer. Within seventy-five days they pulled back the New Coke and reverted to the regular version.

Whatever your decision will be, the key to your success will be continuity:

- Continuity in your marketing message
- Continuity in the quality you deliver
- Continuity in your customer care
- Continuity in your creativity

Continuity means that all you do has a coordinated look and feel. The words and colors you use should be consistent and clearly present throughout your unique selling proposition. This could be defined as your corporate identity, and can apply even to the smallest business. If you want to become big, act big. Give yourself the tools the "big guys" are using. You also want to train your teams into using the same verbiage when presenting your new venture/products/offer.

Finally, you will need to come up with a new tag line: a short sentence that will unmistakably make your potential clients think about your company when they face a burning need that your products can satisfy.

Homework

- Brainstorm and come up with a new tag line for your new brand if necessary, or to represent your new company positioning.
- Define a consistent or continuous marketing strategy, including corporate identity and team-training.

Your Resources

You have settled on your brand and product strategy. You know your market and your end customer. Now, you need to send out your troops to carry the corporate word to the world.

Greg Norman

"Our success is a direct result of knowing how to market a brad and having the right people representing the brand."

If you have decided to keep the two existing brands side-by-side, then you will not need to change your teams, though you will need to train them into knowing what the other side of the company is selling. Your team, from top to bottom, should know by heart what your product catalog lists and what the respective advantages of each product are. If you have personnel interacting with the outside world, like the media, for instance, brief them so that they can address a skeptical community, who may not understand your strategy and may question your decisions. In any case, your teams need to act as if the strategy is the best given the circumstances and that they have no doubt about it.

If you decide to merge your brands into one, you will need to:

1. Communicate tirelessly on this decision with your teams. They need to buy into your decision. You cannot impose it against their will or they will lack motivation, which could result in a loss of precious market share.

Even better, make your teams understand that your decision was based in part on looking out for their best interests.

2. **Train your teams.** From manufacturing to marketing to customer support, they all need to know: What's new, what is not true anymore, why you are now stronger than before, what makes you the leader in your market. Make sure all team members do not refer to the past as the "lost golden age," as this would be counterproductive. This is often seen in mergers or joint ventures. When Hewlett-Packard merged with Compaq, I heard people from Hewlett-Packard criticizing the new ways and fighting as much as they could to keep their old ways. Needless to say, those attitudes do not support an aggressive and efficient new branding strategy. Hence, training and communication are fundamental.

3. **Hire new key positions for your new product/brand plan.** This will guarantee you create yourself a team of employees who are not longing for lost times. These new people should not be mingled in all teams but rather be the new blood of your tactical plan and hence, create their own group.

Your Public Relations and Marketing Plan

If your marketing budget is on a shoestring, then well-built public relations is your golden path. With good public relations, there is no need to invest in advertising, pay-per-click programs and other expensive approaches.

Let's review your eight different possible venues, from least expensive to most expensive:

1. Be found: optimized website (free)
2. Be distributed: viral marketing and affiliate programs (free)
3. Be considered as the reference: write articles (free)
4. Be presented: media coverage (free or basic publicist cost)
5. Be found 100% of the time: pay-per-click (costs can run very high)
6. Be everywhere: flyers, ads in magazines, online banners (higher)
7. Be endorsed: hire a celebrity figure (very expensive)
8. Be heard and seen: advertising on TV, radio (the most expensive)
9. Be Found: Optimized Website (Free)

While large corporations with unlimited marketing budgets can use all of the above, you may have to decide where to allocate your precious resources. If you belong to the 85% of businesses with a website, start with the obvious. Hire a web marketing coach on top of your graphic designer (a designer possesses necessary skills for building a website but their primary objective is to make your site look good) and work on your keywords, inbound links, anchors, etc. Beware of search engine spamming. The Googles and Yahoo!s of this world have strict guidelines when it comes to spammers, and you may end up being banned forever. Search engine spamming is when you use more keywords than necessary (e.g. 100 times on one page), if you use link farms (artificial links to your site), or too many meaningless anchors. If you don't have the budget to hire an expert, follow your common sense and work on the structure of your site that includes easy navigation, a nice balance between non-keywords and keywords, and meaningful anchors within the site.

> **Beware**
>
> Some websites claim to be able to bring you to a top-ten search engine ranking overnight for your keywords. Note that there is never such a certainty as search engines fine-tune their algorithms on a regular basis. Some of them have included extra elements in their ranking method (age of the site, how long was it registered, etc.). Do not waste your hard-earned cash on those hoaxes. Instead, go for reputable resources.

Be Distributed: Viral Marketing and Affiliate Programs (Free)

This is a dream come true. Today you can get promoted to thousands of new clients; millions even, without having to pay anything up-front! This is achieved thanks to affiliate programs.

There is no need for a fancy home-developed program. Nowadays, the vast majority of online shopping cart programs offer this tool for a small monthly fee (about $50/month). This will allow you to market your catalog to clients you would never have reached otherwise. Affiliates are highly motivated salespeople, but you don't need to pay them a monthly retainer. Their earnings are 100% sales-based. Help your affiliates market your products better by creating inviting banners and promotional texts. Create special offers: limited time, limited quantity, etc. To motivate your affiliates even more, make sure you offer a 365-day cookie limit, or as I have seen on the market, no-time limit. Just make sure you have a disclaimer covering you in case your affiliate program provider goes under, or if your company changes strategy and decides to terminate all affiliate relationships, etc. This will allow your affiliates to earn commissions on subsequent sales from an original buyer without having to generate a sale on their own site.

An example is the strategy we used at MyPrivateCoach.com. We decided to start an affiliate program very early on when we only had four coaches on board and twelve programs to sell. Slowly but surely we built up a faithful and motivated affiliate base which has been promoting our coaching program around the globe. This is how we got our first clients in untapped markets like Vietnam and in the Fiji Islands.

With affiliates, you can expect to grow your business at a faster pace, in a larger geographical area than you could reach by yourself, and at a higher rate than you initially planned.

With affiliates in place, you can change your brand effortlessly. You just need to inform your resellers as well, as your teams and customers. It will only require communication and the creation of new banners from your side.

Another free way to expand your market reach is viral marketing. Viral means your message will get propagated in an unplanned and uncontrollable way. The flip side of this is that you reach out to hundreds of thousands of viewers and readers. The higher your pass-along rate, the more people you will reach and the more potential buyers you will attain. Think of this concept as a growing snowball. If you have one thousand people in your subscriber base, 30% of whom pass your E-mail along, and then out of those, another 20% pass along, etc., you can easily calculate how many people you can reach in no time and with very little effort.

The best way to have viral marketing work for you is to:

- Create an audio clip
- Create a video clip
- Write a white paper (a solution-based information article)
- Write an article
- Send out periodic tips and tricks

The idea is that whatever you create is perceived as having such value that it needs to be shared. The top shared material (after pornographic freebies) is funny videos and animations. Be careful; although this is propagating very fast, presenting your new brand in a funny way may impair your future marketing strategy.

Writing information-rich white papers or articles which can be distributed is an amazing way to reach out to your potential customers. If you help them learn something, you will be remembered as the company to trust when in need. Don't forget that good white papers and articles get read by the press too, so you may end up hitting two birds with one stone.

Another powerful way to build a base of faithful customers who will forward your E-mails is to send out newsletters and periodic tips and tricks where the recipient feels he is learning something useful. Make sure you have the "forward me" link at the bottom of all your correspondence to your subscribers.

Try to produce all of the above. This may sound like a daunting task, but with the right planning and resources it is not. Go progressively from what you feel completely comfortable producing (an article, for example) to what is most foreign to you (possibly a video). You will learn in the process and bring in more potential clients.

Remember, integrity is essential, so make sure you own all the rights on what you send out (images, texts, videos and audios).

Be Considered as the Reference: Write Articles and Books (Free)

You changed brands; you added new products to your catalog; you may even have changed your corporate identity; but there is one thing you don't want to change; it is your status as the reference (or expert) in your industry.

Your company can be the reference, or better, you as a person. If readers can identify themselves to you, you will gain their trust. Trust takes time to build, but it is a fundamental building block of your market share. If you are John Doe, in other words, unknown at this point, whether your product is called SuperTurbo or SpamJik, you are still you and you can still be a reference for your industry.

The best-recognized way to achieve such a status is to publish articles, books and other papers.

Publish your articles on your own website with an author box. Allow publishing so long as the author box is kept intact. The author box will contain all your contact information and well as a direct link to your site. When you feel an article deserves high recognition, send it to your contacts in the media world. Have it listed in article directories, and accept speaking engagements in your field.

Publish a book. It is easier than you think! If you have the material but don't feel like hunting down an agent or a publisher, self-publish it. With the new kids on the block of publishing, you are guaranteed instant success if your book is dynamite. Not only will your "baby" get printed and distributed, not to mention be available through online book retailers, but also you will be approached by "regular" mainstream publishers. This will further support your positioning as a reference in your field, thereby helping position your company and its products (whichever brand they carry).

Be Presented: Media Coverage (Free or Basic Publicist Cost)

Being featured on a national newspaper, magazine or invited to a prime time TV show will propel you and your brand to the top. Your sales will skyrocket in no time. Your brand (old or new) will be exposed to millions of potential buyers. Make sure you can absorb a drastic increase in sales volume, as a dissatisfied client who cannot be delivered to is not your end goal!

There are zillions of "how to" books on the market that teach how to "attack" the media market, but no need for 120 pages because the rules are simple:

- **You need a story.** Journalists are constantly solicited. They receive hundreds of E-mails a day. You need to grab the journalist's attention in your first sentence. Show you have read her articles. Explain why you thought about contacting her and why your story is, in fact, a gem. Do your homework first, and scan all major publications and TV shows that could benefit from having you or your company featured.
- **You need some newsworthy element.** Did you release a new product? Do you want to bring your joint venture to the public? Do you want to explain your new brand or your new positioning?
- **Tap into your network.** With the six-level rule, you will be able to reach almost whomever you need to get in touch with. If you are a beginner in the media arena, start low and don't ask to be connected to the top guys right away. You want to learn on a local TV or with a local newspaper; not live with Larry King, Oprah, or in The New York Times.
- **You need to follow up.** Have you contacted a journalist with no answer? Follow up the week after, and then ten days later. After a few contacts, if nothing happens, stop and keep this contact for later. Do not waste your time and do not appear as a "pest." If you get an answer, then follow up until a real relationship is created. Do not expect journalists to write "nice" articles about you. They are, usually, honest people who write/present what will serve their readers or viewers. But if your story is compelling, you will get great coverage. For instance, if you joined forces with the Goliath of the industry and you were David, then people will want to understand how you did it and what's in it for you and for them as potential clients. If you started from nothing, your story is even better from a journalistic perspective. All this coverage will serve your brand positioning.
- **Stay in touch.** For those cold leads, keep in contact regularly. Send them press releases and share stories and article ideas with them on a monthly basis. Very soon you will become an obvious player in their landscape.

- **Change strategy.** If your media strategy is not working, then fine-tune it: change your story, change your timing, your media targets, etc. until you find the right angle. There is no miraculous recipe, but there will be results for the motivated joint venturer.
- **Publish press releases.** One of the key tools for being noticed and getting your word out is the use of press releases. Aim for one press release per month. Be visible constantly. Send those press releases to all your contacts. You can expect viral marketing to kick in, as some of them will pass this along to others. And who knows? Your E-mail may end up on Larry King's desk!
- **Keep faith.** At times when you have a hard time selling yourself, your story or your brand to media people, you may feel it is hopeless. Don't! Stay strong and fine-tune your strategy until you have found the right angle.

The cost for PR can go from zero (you or your team do it) to thousands of dollars, depending on the publicist you hire. Selecting the right publicist is a delicate task, as there are dozens of thousands of publicists on the market who have no track record at all or who will adamantly claim that they cannot guarantee any results. You are better off asking your advisors (remember, advisors are sitting on your advisory board and can be trusted) or other entrepreneurs like you for references. Do not rely on a nice website to make your decision. Meet with your publicist face to face, ask for track record and ask to talk to former clients. Keep your costs low for the first three months.

> **Beware**
> - Some publicists, even reputable ones, are in the business of selling their services, not necessarily getting you results. Often they will promise TV, radio, and other types of exposure, but you must find out exactly what they are promising and at what price.
> - You could easily find yourself in a situation where only very expensive services will yield any useful exposure. And even then, there is no guarantee.
> - I was extremely lucky early on in my business to avoid some of the pitfalls that are prevalent in this industry.
> - I have also been fortunate enough to find a real gem of a publicist that has done many wonderful projects for me.

Be Found 100% of the Time: Pay-Per-Click (Costs Can Run Very High)

Pay-per-click is the purchase of sponsored links on the result pages of search engines. The principle is simple: you bid for your keywords (example, business coaching) and the higher bidder gets the first place on the page.

The main players in this field are Google AdWords, Yahoo! Search Marketing (includes Overture), MSN Paid Listings, AskJeeves, and Mama.

There are obvious advantages and drawbacks on a pay-per-click campaign:

- **Advantage #1: Market Reach.** Being at the top of the list will guarantee increased traffic to your site and will allow you to reach a larger number of potential buyers. This helps you gain an advantage in trying to compete in highly competitive industries where it is extremely difficult to reach the top of the list (for example: weight loss). This will also help you pump up your subscribers list should you focus your efforts on this.
- **Advantage #2: Speed.** While you optimize your joint venture website or your new brand pages, buying sponsored links will save time and allow you to stay at the top of the results as you improve your organic ranking.
- **Advantage #3: Trackability.** You will be able to evaluate your ROI with a high level of confidence. The main players in this field all provide you with tracking tools. These are critical as they help you constantly fine-tune your keywords and your landing pages.
- **Advantage #4: Controlled Costs.** You can control (cap) how much you are willing to spend on a particular campaign. Most search engines offer you the ability to put a limit per keyword phrases, per day, per month or per theme.
- **Advantage #5: Trial and Error.** Since a pay-per-click campaign is easy to set up and fast to launch, you can use it to test new keyword phrases before launching a full-scale website optimization campaign, which is very costly and time-consuming.
- **Drawback #1: Uncertainty.** While there are obvious markets on which these campaigns will work, be prepared to "not know" in advance what your results will be. This may be stressful and resource-consuming if you are in the middle of a product or a new brand launch. Make sure you allocate enough resources to transform this into a successful experience.
- **Drawback #2: Return on Investment.** One major temptation you may be confronted with as you unroll your pay-per-click campaign is to continue to bet using a "casino style" approach. You bet until you win, except in this world it may

never happen. There are markets and products for which pay-per-clicks don't work: high ticket items, for instance. Would you buy a car via a sponsored link?
- **Drawback #3: Time.** Be careful not to spend too much time constantly analyzing your ad campaign. This will be a temptation. Whether you lose or make money, you will want to understand how to make more or how to stop wasting your hard-earned cash. However, be prepared to have tracking tools to fully understand the process and your ROI.

Homework
- Conduct an in-depth keyword analysis. This is not as straightforward as it seems, and you may need to consult with an expert in the field.
- Select your products to be marketed first.
- Define your budget and set up your campaign with appropriate limits.
- Fine-tune and test, test, test.
- Based on your campaign ROI, extend, modify, or roll out a new campaign.

Be Everywhere: Flyers, Ads in Magazines, Online Banners (Higher)

If your marketing budget allows it, buying exposure in targeted media (USA Today, Los Angeles Times or any other mainstream national newspaper, for instance) will help carry your word to millions of readers.

In the order of cost from less to more expensive are online banners, flyers and advertisements in magazines and newspapers. Take great care in defining your strategy, as you will not be able to fine-tune this ad campaign as you go. Once your banner has been sent to the magazines, website, or newspaper, you cannot change it; at least not without some difficulty.

The cost can range from a few hundred dollars to over $100,000 for a full page in a national newspaper, for example. Cost-effective flyers may work well in your local markets or at industry events. With online design and printing, you can very easily get thousands of flyers for less than $300. Read a white paper on ROI for these types of approaches. Ask experts, and hire consultants to get expert information. In short, do your homework before putting large amounts of cash down the drain.

You can handle this activity in-house or outsource it to specialized companies with a proven track record.

Be Endorsed: Hire a Celebrity Figure (Very Expensive)

Having a celebrity endorse your product, your company, or your latest book is an amazing business propeller.

There are several ways to achieve this goal. Hiring a publicist whom you know is celebrity-savvy, and sending material to each targeted celebrity's agent or publicist. Remember, these people are constantly bombarded with similar demands, so work well on your mailer before sending it out. This is your baby. You only get one shot at it. Find what that celebrity is interested in and write about it in your letter. If you have a story that might capture this star's attention, present it in an aggressive way where your keywords are bold and in strong colors (red, for instance). If you have nice T-shirts to promote your brand, send them out. You never know, Madonna may end up wearing it!

This can seem like a long shot. However, Michael Scadden, Business Coach at MyPrivateCoach.com, likes to cite the following anecdote: One of his clients was opening up a spa in a joint venture format with two experts from different backgrounds. She was looking for a way to increase the visibility of her fancy spa to be the only alternative people would think of when needing an Ayurvedic massage. Michael found an article where a national superstar athlete explained at length why Ayurvedic massage had changed his life. She simply reproduced the article in a larger format and put it in a conspicuous place in the lobby of her business for her customers to see. This indirect endorsement worked almost as well as a direct one for a cost next to zero (the cost for enlarged photocopies).

Be Heard and Seen: Advertising on TV, Radio (Most Expensive)

In the case of large joint ventures and when large marketing budgets are allocated to the promotion of the venture, new lines of products or of new brands, TV and radio ads are a sure way to go.

National TV prime time seconds are the most costly while local radio mid-day ads are the cheapest. You will need to consult with an expert in this field and conduct extensive analysis as to which channel, what time, and which program would benefit you most.

> **Beware**
>
> As you become more famous in your field, you may be approached by companies who claim they can get you on TV. You must know that TV channels will never contact you directly to advertise on their channel unless you are a "big guy" (Coca-Cola, for instance). Most likely you will have been contacted by an infomercial company, which markets $25,000 segments. Unless there is a clear track record indicating infomercials work for your target market, stay away!

As you have seen, your brand is your most valuable asset, and you want to treat it very carefully when you join forces with another player in your market.

Your homework in this chapter is heavier than in others, because you cannot make mistakes when it comes to your trade name. One error may take you months or years to recover. Take the time to talk to experts and consultants who come highly recommended. Allocate the appropriate resources to conduct in-depth analyses and be ready to swing back quickly if your decision proves wrong. Remember that it is most detrimental to your business if you refuse to accept your error and are unwilling to change paths.

That said, hundreds and thousands of businesses are successfully joining forces, changing their brand and prosperously growing. Now it's your turn!

Chapter 7 Highlights

- Once you have decided which brand to keep or develop you will need to evaluate your in-house marketing and PR resources.
- Establish a marketing plan and budget and select the three or four top goals you want to accomplish: Be found (optimized website), be distributed (viral marketing and affiliate programs), be considered as the reference (write articles and books), be presented (media coverage), be found 100% of the time (pay-per-click), be everywhere (flyers, ads in magazines, online banners), be endorsed (celebrity figures), be heard and seen: (advertising on TV, radio).
- Remember to remain "tough" as you become more "famous," for there is a 100% guarantee that you will be approached by unethical marketers who will promise you the moon for a few hundred thousand dollars. It is hard to not fall for some of those tricks, so just keep in mind to beware of "too-good-to-be-true" offers.

chapter 8
Exit Strategies - The End

Joint ventures are created to serve a specific business purpose. In the Joint Venture Agreement, you should have a clearly defined exit strategy. Getting out of such a partnership without getting hurt is essential to a healthy relationship with your partners in business. Additionally, you should have a clear objective when it comes to exit strategies right from the start. Several planned exit strategies exist.

They are:

1. A future merger with one of the joint venture's parent entities
2. Merging with another entity
3. Initial public offering (going public with your business)

Being Acquired by a Parent Company

The companies involved in a joint venture have the ability to merge with one of the parent companies if one exists.

Large corporations start joint venture projects for many reasons: testing of a new idea, a new concept, distribution in hard-to-reach countries, injection of new blood in their large structures, acquisition of new technologies, etc. Depending on their high-level strategic direction, they may want to bring this success back into their full control. In that case, this may mean the end of the start-up mentality for the joint venture. Various scenarios include a complete acquisition of both the company and its products/services, or a partial acquisition where the parent company may choose to retain portions of the original joint venture. The other half of the joint venture, which does not have a connection to the acquiring parent company, may also choose to buy out products/services it feels are valuable and slowly integrate them into other lines. Eventually, there will be the complete disappearance of the joint venture as it was known.

Merging With Another Entity

As the joint venture becomes a market player, it may attract the attention of:

- Direct competitors who want to eliminate this threat and expand their market reach (as well as acquire new technologies and intellectual property).
- Other market players who are pursuing a vertical development and want to occupy this market position.
- The joint venture management itself can decide to expand and/or hold a position in a market segment (vertical or horizontal) which it does not cover yet.
- Wherever the decision comes from, it will lead to a thorough evaluation of the joint venture and the other entity (each company will order the evaluation of the other).

Initial Public Offering (Going Public With Your Business)

Congratulations! You have achieved your goal! You now belong to the powerful group of successful joint venturers. Your results are fantastic, and you have become a key player in your industry. You want to expand further and need to raise some public funding, you may have investors who wish to recoup their investment with an IPO, or though you can still grow without injecting any fresh cash in the company, you want to transform your market success into a stellar stock exchange success and retire earlier than planned.

If you answered yes to any of the above, then an IPO is the premier exit strategy. To do an IPO in the best conditions, you will need to:

- Generate at least $100 million in revenues (or replace the revenue part by a very large high-quality subscriber database à la Skype).
- Have healthy margins for your industry and line of trade.
- Show high growth potential.
- Have clear accounting books with no fuzzy international gimmicks or questionable tax loopholes.
- Have at least five years in business.
- Choose a top investment bank to support your IPO process.
- Accept opening up your capital and lose the control of your entity.
- Have the agreement of the major joint venture partners.

Doing an IPO is not a miracle, it is rather a dream that can come true if you do your homework correctly, work hard, find the right partners and make the right decisions. Not all companies, even successful ones, decide to do an IPO, although it is the most certain path to early retirement. To make sure this is what you and your joint venture needs, I suggest you meet with an investment banker and a corporate lawyer to understand all the implications a public offering can have.

Write a SWOT analysis (Strengths, Weaknesses, Opportunities and Threats) to help you determine what's best for you. Force yourself to fill in all the empty fields to cover all the ground and uncover hidden or ill-understood traps.

Share your findings with your advisory board (if you have one), people you trust, and successful joint venturers. In the end, you are the one to reach the conclusion, but getting outside feedback will comfort you in your decision.

Unplanned Circumstances

There are also unplanned circumstances that could result in the end of your joint venture. The best way to avoid the effects of these is to understand that they are possible and plan for these contingencies. If they are not planned for in the formal agreement, you should at least be aware of some of them.

A partial list includes:

1. Sickness or death of one or more of the partners
2. Disagreement between the parties
3. The joint venture missed its target (did not achieve its intended goal)

Sickness or Death of One or More of the Partners

Although unfortunate and usually unforeseen at the beginning of a joint venture, contingencies should be put in place for the possibility of interruption and/or inactivity due to death or sickness of one or more of the partners.

In the event of death, it should be clearly defined how the structure of a joint venture will function if there is a transfer of ownership. If nothing has been put in agreement for such an event, unfortunate or unbearable circumstances can result. For example, depending on the legal entities of the companies involved in a joint venture, it is possible and not uncommon that spouses or heirs of the deceased will take over ownership of the joint venture.

Properly planning for such an event, though unpleasant, is necessary. Often agreements consist of the non-deceased party having the "right of first refusal" to buy out the shares of the deceased individual. Since value is difficult to determine in the beginning, clauses in the joint venture usually include verbiage such as "Fair Market Value" for understanding the true valuation of the joint venture at the time of death. Normally, a third party assessor (usually a CPA) will perform an audit of the business, and the surviving party will purchase the shares of the deceased by paying his or her estate and then assume full control of the joint venture.

Of course there are other methods to divide a company, but this is the most common

Sickness or Incapacitation

Sickness or incapacitation of one or more of the partners at times can become an issue. Though no one's fault, feelings of anger or frustration can arise if this has not been properly planned for. Some of the issues involve:

- Feelings of guilt from the incapacitated party over not being able to contribute
- Anger from the non-incapacitated party over having to work harder without there necessarily being any extra reward
- Determining equitable splits during periods of absence

In dealing with these possibilities, it is best to set up in advance well defined roles and value for those roles. In the case of two owners coming together to form a joint venture, those owners may assume several roles in the business. These roles may include:

1. Chairperson
2. CEO, CFO, CTO, etc.
3. Business Development
4. Sales
5. Technician

Wearing these different hats, as we say, has values above and beyond being owners of the company. If one or more roles are assumed by the individual who is ill, the other partner, members of the team, or possibly additions to your workforce, will have to be considered to make up for the void left by that individual.

Assigning a value to these positions can allow the owners of the business to easily determine the loss and consequences of such an occurrence.

Disagreement Between the Parties

When partners have irreconcilable points of view which prevent the joint venture from reaching its goals, the decision is often made to terminate the partnership. If this event was mentioned and structured in the joint venture agreement, then you will only need to use a lawyer to help you draft a Notice of Joint Venture Termination (two or three short paragraphs). This notice will have to be signed by all parties involved and will list the following:

1. Reasons for termination
2. Existing assets allocation between parties
3. Intellectual property ownership
4. If relevant, employees' termination

In the event of a sale of the assets to different entities, (computer, intellectual property, software, inventory, etc.), you will need to list this in the notice as well.

Irreconcilable points of view (i.e. a situation with no possible exit) can be loss of trust in one of the parties, and/or complete lack of common ground when it comes to business planning and strategy. If the departure of one partner puts the joint venture at risk, the remaining partners can decide to terminate their collaboration in the event that the lack of one profile will prevent the joint venture from being a success.

This workable exit strategy is a critical factor of success for maintaining a chance for the partners to one day work together again, or for you to learn from this apparent failure and start again. Going through this process will probably better prepare you for the next venture.

The Joint Venture Missed Its Target (Did Not Achieve Its Intended Goal)

Despite all our hopes and goals at the beginning of the joint venture, often we will not accomplish what we set out to achieve. While it is true that most businesses fail (90-95%); who actually enters the winners' circle is a question mark.

Diligence in your preparation prior to business launch, putting the right systems and people in place, and, of course, old-fashioned hard work can greatly increase your chances of being a success. However, even under the best of conditions, you may fall short of your intended target.

In these cases, it is best not to hold on, creating more losses and wasted time. It is easy to become emotionally attached to your business, "your baby" as some call it, but this is a huge mistake. Learn to know when to quit. There is no sense in getting deeper into trouble if there is little or no hope of survival. Besides, the beautiful thing about business is that you can always attempt it again at some point.

In the end, try to get what you can from it. If there are no monetary rewards, often you gain in knowledge which can serve you later. The experience you will undoubtedly get from the venture will be invaluable. Not even a college education can equal the "hands-on" experience of running your own business or being a part of a Joint Venture.

If there is anything left of the business (office equipment, intellectual property, residual cash/assets, etc.), dividing them by what the partners feel is an equal split is a simple matter. Try to avoid petty arguments, as this might lead to legal intervention. It is my experience that when this happens, everyone loses except for the lawyers. Often, your time is far too valuable to be caught up in these activities that are costly not only in terms of financial loss, but also as stressful energy drainers.

Try to move on quickly and let go of any residual anger or feelings of loss or despair. Remember, another business can be just around the corner; only this time you are more skilled and are better prepared for success.

Conclusion

Owning a business can be one of the most exciting times in one's career. If done correctly, it can create the dream life you have always wanted. Depending on what you want from your business and how fast you want to get there, joining forces to create a more powerful presence in your market may be an attractive option.

As with any business, there are risks, but by following the proven steps in the book, you greatly increase your chances of success. Although the information in this work won't change the national statistics on successful ventures, our hope is that it will greatly determine who in fact does succeed.

You now have the most powerful information available from start to finish on conceiving, starting, running and ultimately producing a top notch joint venture. Now it is up to you to get started. Remember, you are not alone. If you are still hesitant in any way, feel free to contact me at www.myprivatecoach.com. We have many experts that can help give you the confidence boost you need to get started and help keep you on track with your goals.

The only thing stopping you now is you. No more excuses! Get out there, get to work and pave the way to your success.

I am proud to be a part of your journey.

appendix A
List of Outside Resources

All along this book I have mentioned useful resources that may help you reach your goals in the joint-venture world:

Websites:
- http://www.MyPrivateCoach.com: the #1 coaching organization in North America and in Europe
- http://biztaxlaw.about.com: extensive information on business law for US-based companies
- http://ecnow.com/Internet_Marketing.htm: 35+ Internet Marketing techniques
- http://www.MarketingSherpa.com: Great marketing articles and information
- http://www.hbsp.harvard.edu/b02/en/hbr/hbr_current_issue.jhtml: Harvard Business Review
- http://www.hr-guide.com/selection.htm: HR Guide
- http://www.FindLaw.com: great resource for free templates (joint venture agreement for instance)
- http://www.30daybootcamp.com: online coaching programs

- http://www.law.cornell.edu/wex/index.php/Category: from prestigious Cornell Law School, a wealth of constantly updated legal information
- http://www.marketingpower.com: American Marketing Association
- http://www.linkedin.com: the #1 online social and professional network
- http://www.constantcontact.com: an email campaign generator for non HTML savvy entrepreneurs
- http://www.wikipedia.com: an online free encyclopedia which was recently rated as good as Encyclopedia Britannica
- http://www.sourceforge.org: a source for freeware for the cost-conscious joint-venturer
- http://management.about.com/cs/adminaccounting/a/teambuilding.htm?terms=team+building: a very well written article on team building
- http://www.shrm.org: Society for Human Resources Management
- http://www.Hewitt.com: A global HR outsourcing and consulting firm

Books:
- "*Everyday Employment Law: The Basics*" by Amy DelPo and Lisa Guerin
- "*Give Me a Break*" by John Stossel
- "*Harvard Business Review on Entrepreneurship*" (Harvard Business Review Paperback Series) (Paperback) by Amar Bhldt, William Sahlman, James Stancil, Arthur Rock, Michael Nevens, Gregory Summe

- "*Guerrilla Marketing: Secrets for Making Big Profits from Your Small Business*" (Guerrilla Marketing) (Paperback) by Jay Conrad Levinson
- "*The 22 Immutable Laws of Branding*" (Paperback) by Al Ries, Laura Ries

- Publisher: Happy About (http://happyabout.info), mitchell.levy@happyabout.info, 408-257-3000

NOTE Document templates available at http://HappyAbout.info/jointventuring/

About the Author

Valerie Orsoni-Vauthey is the CEO and Founder of MyPrivateCoach.com, a leading USA and European coaching organization. Her experience in banking and venture capital has allowed her to participate in a number of successful joint-ventures, including: one in the artificial intelligence field (sold), one in the online retailing business (sold), and one in the online services world (30dayBootCamp.com). She is a regular guest on the Good Life Show, invited on business radio shows in Europe and frequently interviewed by the press.

She can be reached at happyabout@myprivatecoach.com

www.ingramcontent.com/pod-product-compliance
Ingram Content Group UK Ltd.
Pitfield, Milton Keynes, MK11 3LW, UK
UKHW041419180426
11947UKWH00007B/208